Dearest Christina,

Might this book bring enlightenment and blessing to you.

dearly,

& Dad

March, 2011

RANDY ALCORN

90 Days
of God's
Goodness

Daily Reflections

That Shine Light *on* Personal Darkness

MULTNOMAH
BOOKS

Ninety Days of God's Goodness
Published by Multnomah Books
12265 Oracle Boulevard, Suite 200
Colorado Springs, Colorado 80921

ISBN 978-1-60142-344-3
ISBN 978-1-60142-354-2 (electronic)

Library of Congress Cataloging-in-Publication Data
Alcorn, Randy C.
    Ninety days of God's goodness : daily reflections that shine light on personal darkness / Randy Alcorn.— 1st ed.
        p. cm.
    ISBN 978-1-60142-344-3—ISBN 978-1-60142-354-2 (electronic)
1. Suffering—Religious aspects—Christianity—Meditations. 2. God (Christianity)—Goodness—Meditations. 3. Bible—Meditations. 4. Meditations. I. Title.
    BV4909.A277 2011
    242'.4—dc22
                                          2010033427

Printed in the United States of America
2011—First Edition

10 9 8 7 6 5 4 3 2 1

Nanci and I are honored to dedicate this book to our beloved sister
Sono Harris
(resided here 1954–2010; now living with Jesus)
World-class daughter to Lily
Gold medal wife to Gregg
Hall of Fame mother to Josh, Joel, Alex, Brett, Sarah, Isaac, and James
Sono, you are precious beyond words.
Yours was one of the best-lived and most unforgettable lives Nanci and
I have ever witnessed. God graciously endowed you with wisdom,
insight, heart, class, purpose, and joy. The heritage you left your family,
and the rest of us, is stunning in its breadth and depth. Your destiny is
to shine in God's presence "like the brightness of the heavens…like the
stars for ever and ever" (Daniel 12:3). No small providence!
Thank you, Jesus, for your overflowing work of grace in our sister's
life. And thank you, Sono, for your example to us and our daughters,
all the way back to those ballet lessons twenty-five years ago. Even
your e-mails, expressing thoughts and prayers as I wrote my books
and blogged, were worth framing.
Sono, we have been touched deeply by your faithfulness to our Lord and
your service to your family and Christ's church. We can't wait to see you
again in a far better world. On the New Earth we would be honored to
serve our glorious King under your leadership.

Special thanks to Doreen Button for her assistance in
selecting additional Scripture passages and helping arrange what I
wrote; and to Doreen, Steve Tucker, Thomas Womack, and Pam
Shoup for their editorial advice at various stages of the process. Thanks
also to Ken Petersen, who encouraged me to pursue this project.

Introduction

A Journey Toward Jesus

Now that same day two of them were going to a village called Emmaus, about seven miles from Jerusalem. They were talking with each other about everything that had happened. As they talked and discussed these things with each other, Jesus himself came up and walked along with them; but they were kept from recognizing him.…

As they approached the village to which they were going, Jesus acted as if he were going farther. But they urged him strongly, "Stay with us, for it is nearly evening; the day is almost over." So he went in to stay with them.

When he was at the table with them, he took bread, gave thanks, broke it and began to give it to them. Then their eyes were opened and they recognized him, and he disappeared from their sight. They asked each other, "Were not our hearts burning within us while he talked with us on the road and opened the Scriptures to us?"

—LUKE 24:13–16, 28–32

I magine eavesdropping on the conversation between Jesus and these two disciples. Consider the questions they may have asked and the answers he gave. One day in Heaven, I want to see the video!

I'll bet at least one of their questions related to that which looms large for most who read this book: If God is good...*why all this evil and suffering?* If God loves us, how can he justify allowing (or sending) the sometimes overwhelming difficulties we face?

I invite you to join me on a journey to discover what God has to say about this subject. I can't think of a better way to do this than by daily meditating on his Word. I've ended each meditation with a brief prayer, written from my heart. Perhaps my prayer will echo yours, or perhaps it will prompt for you a renewed conversation with God.

While exploring God's goodness in the midst of a suffering world, I've taken the most pleasure in focusing on him, exploring his attributes of goodness, love, holiness, justice, patience, grace, and mercy. Although I haven't unearthed easy answers, I'm astonished at how much insight the Bible offers.

I've beheld a God who says, "I have indeed seen the misery of my people in Egypt. I have heard them crying out because of their slave drivers, and I am concerned about their suffering" (Exodus 3:7). I've found great comfort in hearing God speak of a time when he could bear his people's misery no longer (see Judges 10:16). I revel in God's emphatic promise that he will make a New Earth, where he will come down to live with us and on which "he will wipe every tear from their eyes. There will be no more death or mourning or crying or pain" (Revelation 21:4).

Above all, in the process of meditating on this subject and writing this book, I've seen Jesus.

The first physician to die of the AIDS virus in the United Kingdom was a young Christian. He contracted the disease while conducting medical research in Zimbabwe. In the last days of his life, he struggled to express himself to his wife. Near the end, he couldn't talk and had only enough strength to write the letter *J*. She ran through her mental dictionary, saying various words beginning with *J*. None was right. Finally she said, "Jesus?"

He nodded. Yes, Jesus.[1]

Jesus filled his thoughts. That's all he wanted to say. That's all his wife needed to know.

In the end, that's all each of us needs to know.

Lord, I so look forward to having conversations with you where I not only ask questions but, like those disciples on the Emmaus road, also hear answers from your own mouth! I'm grateful there's no need to envy the disciples, because one day I, too, will walk with you in a resurrected body, and you will open the Scriptures to me, and at last I will understand so much of what eludes me now. But until then, thank you that you are not silent! You've provided your Word, your Holy Spirit, and your people to help me understand—and grace to trust you when I don't.

I

Conflict with a Purpose

Then Joseph said to his brothers, "Come close to me." When they had done so, he said, "I am your brother Joseph, the one you sold into Egypt! And now, do not be distressed and do not be angry with yourselves for selling me here, because it was to save lives that God sent me ahead of you. For two years now there has been famine in the land, and for the next five years there will not be plowing and reaping. But God sent me ahead of you to preserve for you a remnant on earth and to save your lives by a great deliverance.

"So then, it was not you who sent me here, but God. He made me father to Pharaoh, lord of his entire household and ruler of all Egypt....

"You intended to harm me, but God intended it for good to accomplish what is now being done, the saving of many lives."

—GENESIS 45:4–8; 50:20

After Job had prayed for his friends, the LORD made him prosperous again and gave him twice as much as he had before. All his brothers and sisters and everyone who had known him before…comforted and consoled him over all the trouble the LORD had brought upon him.…

The LORD blessed the latter part of Job's life more than the first.

—JOB 42:10–12

While most of my books are nonfiction, I've written seven full-length novels. Now, if I were to write a novel about lives without conflict, where characters get everything they want, where life marches on comfortably and no one ever loses anything, nobody would read it. Who likes a boring story? In fact, my central characters always face great conflict, turmoil, uncertainty, and suffering. Some die. That it makes for a far better story is my main reason for doing this. (We enjoy in fiction much that we do not enjoy in life.)

So who am I to say that God shouldn't write such things into *his* story, including my part?

In our lives God uses conflict not just to make the story better but to make *us* better. In life, not just literature, we repeatedly see that protection from conflict produces soft, spoiled, and selfish people, while enduring conflict is more likely to produce someone strong, capable, and caring.

If, in an interview with a character from one of my novels, you were to ask whether he'd like to be written out of the story, he would answer no. Nonexistence appeals to no one. Now ask him if he would like to suffer less, and he'll answer yes. Who wouldn't?

I empathize with my characters since I, too, am a character in God's story. At times I'd love to take a break from the drama. Three months off without stress would feel nice. But I also realize I'm part of something great, far bigger than myself. And I trust God not only to bring the whole story together but also to do with my part of it what he knows to be best.

Given the option while facing his trials, I'm confident Joseph would have walked off the stage of God's story. After betrayal by his brothers when he was a teenager and being sold into slavery and later falsely accused by Potiphar's wife and sent to prison, Joseph had surely endured enough for one life!

Talk to Job in the middle of his story—with ten children dead and excruciating boils covering his body, God apparently abandoning him and friends haranguing him. Ask if he wants out. I know what he'd say because he said it: "Why did I not perish at birth?" (Job 3:11).

But that's all over now. On the New Earth, sit by Job and Joseph at a lavish banquet with their Lord. Ask them, "Be honest. *Was it really worth it?*"

"Absolutely," Job says. Joseph smiles, nodding emphatically.

"But, Job, had God given you the choice, wouldn't you have walked out of the story?"

"In a heartbeat. I'm just glad he didn't let me."

You and I are characters in God's story, handmade by him. Every character serves a purpose. God loves a great story, and all of us who know him will recall and celebrate and continue to live in that story for all eternity.

Before we fault him for the plot twists we don't like, we should remember that Jesus has written this story in his own blood.

Father, what a privilege to be chosen by you to be a character in the greatest story ever told—and to know that one day we'll be able to read it start to finish. Thank you for this true, unfolding drama of redemption. Thank you that in the ages to come we will praise you for not letting us walk off the pages. Thank you for accomplishing the purposes in us that at first only you, the Author, understand, but in the end, looking back, we, the readers—and characters—will too.

A Happy Ending with No End

Praise be to the God and Father of our Lord Jesus Christ! In his great mercy he has given us new birth into a living hope through the resurrection of Jesus Christ from the dead, and into an inheritance that can never perish, spoil or fade—kept in heaven for you, who through faith are shielded by God's power until the coming of the salvation that is ready to be revealed in the last time. In this you greatly rejoice, though now for a little while you may have had to suffer grief in all kinds of trials. These have come so that your faith—of greater worth than gold, which perishes even though refined by fire—may be proved genuine and may result in praise, glory and honor when Jesus Christ is revealed. Though you have not seen him, you love him; and even though you do not see him now, you believe in him and are filled with an inexpressible and glorious joy, for you are receiving the goal of your faith, the salvation of your souls.

—1 Peter 1:3–9

We are to rejoice in our inheritance in Heaven even as God sovereignly uses difficulties in our lives as a fire to refine, purify, and strengthen our faith.

I'll never forget my first thirty seconds of high school. I walked in the front door, tripped, and fell on my face…right in front of three cheerleaders. They laughed hysterically. Not a good start for a freshman desperately wanting to be cool!

At the time, that incident hurt worse than my serious ankle injury while playing football. Yet forty years later, even though I still remember it vividly, it brings me absolutely no pain. It just makes me laugh. Of course, my teenage troubles do *not* compare to having cancer, being tortured, or seeing a child die. I only mean that although certain experiences brought me genuine pain when they happened, with the passing of time and gaining of perspective, they no longer do.

If we sometimes recognize this in daily life, shouldn't we suppose that many of our most painful ordeals will look quite different a million years from now as we recall them on the New Earth? What if one day we discover that God wasted *nothing* in our lives on Earth? What if we see that *every* agony was part of giving birth to an eternal joy?

I watched an interview with two families whose daughters, students at Taylor University, suffered a terrible car accident in 2006. A truck hit a van head-on, killing five people.

At the accident scene, someone found Laura Van Ryn's purse next to Whitney Cerak. Workers at the scene mistook the students, both blondes, for each other. Laura, misidentified as Whitney, was pronounced dead at the scene, while Whitney, misidentified as Laura, fought for her life on the way to the hospital. Some fourteen hundred people attended "Whitney's" funeral, and her father spoke at the service. No one suspected that the body they buried that day was Laura Van Ryn's.

For five weeks, the Ceraks believed their daughter had died, while the Van Ryns thought their daughter lived.

When this monumental error finally came to light, both families expressed faith in God. In one conversation, the Ceraks told the Van Ryns, "We are so sorry that we have the happy ending." Don Van Ryn responded, "We do too...we just haven't seen it yet."

The Van Ryns await their reunion with Laura in a better world.

God promises that the eternal ending will break forth in such glorious happiness that all present suffering will pale in comparison. *All* who know Jesus will have a happy ending.

We just haven't seen it yet.

Thank you, Lord, for valuing our faith in you so much that you test and strengthen it through adversity. Thank you for your promise of an unfading inheritance and that you are developing greater Christlikeness in us now that we may be better prepared to rule under you in the eternal kingdom. Though we aren't there yet, we celebrate the fact that because of your grace, we will have a happy ending; one that will never end.

Freedom and Comfort in Truth

I am laid low in the dust;
> preserve my life according to your word.

I recounted my ways and you answered me;
> teach me your decrees.

Let me understand the teaching of your precepts;
> then I will meditate on your wonders.

My soul is weary with sorrow;
> strengthen me according to your word.

Keep me from deceitful ways;
> be gracious to me through your law.

I have chosen the way of truth;
> I have set my heart on your laws.

I hold fast to your statutes, O LORD;
> do not let me be put to shame.

I run in the path of your commands,
> for you have set my heart free.

— PSALM 119:25–32

D on't you love the heartfelt honesty of the words God has chosen to include in the Bible? "My soul is weary with sorrow." It's the burden of life in a hurting world that causes the writer to turn to Scripture for strength: "Preserve my life according to your word.... Strengthen me according to your word."

If abuse, rape, desertion, paralysis, debilitating disease, or the loss of a loved one has devastated you, then the issue of evil and suffering isn't merely theoretical, philosophical, or theological. It's deeply personal. Logical arguments won't satisfy you; in fact, they might offend you. You need help with the emotional problem of evil, not merely the logical problem of evil. Like children at times, each of us must snuggle into our Father's arms, and there receive the comfort we need.

But remember this: you are a whole person. Truth matters. To touch us at the heart level—and to keep touching us over days, months, years, and decades—truth must work its way into our *minds*.

Never seek comfort by ignoring truth. Comfort in falsehood is false comfort. Jesus said, "The truth will set you free" (John 8:32). When you try to soothe your feelings without bothering to think deeply about ideas, you are asking to be manipulated. Quick-fix feelings won't sustain you over the long haul. On the other hand, deeply rooted beliefs—specifically a worldview grounded in Scripture—will allow you to persevere and hold on to a faith built on the solid rock of God's truth.

In writing his magnificent story of redemption, God has revealed truths about himself, us, the world, goodness, evil, suffering, and Heaven and Hell. (I capitalize those terms as proper nouns throughout the book because they are actual places, like New England or Saturn.) Those truths God reveals to us teem with life. The blood of man and God flows through them. God speaks with passion, not indifference; he utters fascinating words, not dull ones. To come to grips with the problem of evil and suffering, you must do more than hear heart-wrenching stories about suffering people. You must hear God's truth to help you interpret those stories.

The Bible reveals him to be a great God, sovereign and all-powerful, gracious and all-good, kind and all-wise. And he is also our Abba, our Papa. But we do not always feel warmth and security, do we?

Maybe you're holding on to years of bitterness and depression. You blame someone for your suffering—and that someone may be God. You will not find relief until you gain perspective. That perspective can be found as you meditate on his wonders and ask him to use the truths of his revealed Word to strengthen you.

Lord, at times my heart is heavy with sorrow. This fallen world isn't an easy place to live in. You know because you descended from Heaven's happiness and lived here, laughed here, suffered here, and were crucified here. Thank you for living as you did and dying as you did and rising as you did so I can live forever with you and your people in a world where you will, once and for all, make all things right.

Honest Faith

My God, my God, why have You forsaken me?
Far from my deliverance are the words of my groaning.
O my God, I cry by day, but You do not answer;
And by night, but I have no rest.
Yet You are holy,
O You who are enthroned upon the praises of Israel.
In You our fathers trusted;
They trusted and You delivered them.
To You they cried out and were delivered;
In You they trusted and were not disappointed.

—PSALM 22:1–5, NASB

W hat an honest cry to God for help: *"Why, God? Why does it seem like you're not answering my prayers?"* As he wrestles with this, David turns to Scripture, where God's deliverance of his people is documented. David reflects on their trust in God. In the end, God's faithfulness to Israel inspires David to believe that God will prove faithful to him as well.

God's Word contains countless expressions of concern and anguish about the hard times people experience and the fact that they sometimes don't feel God's closeness. In this fallen world, "Why?" is a common question.

Randy Butler, a pastor, told me about his teenage son's death. "For twenty years, God gave me a perfect life, family, and ministry. Then Kevin died, and nearly every morning, for three or four months, I screamed questions at God. I asked, 'What were you thinking?' And, 'Is this the best you can do for me?' And finally, 'Do you really expect me to show up every Sunday and tell everyone how great you are?' In the silence I began to hear the voice of God…then, without any announcement, when I became silent, God spoke to my soul. He had an answer for each of my three questions."

Had Randy not been unreservedly honest with God, he couldn't have completely grasped how the God he spoke to had watched his own Son die long before Randy had. God the Father had endured the horrible death of Jesus, his only Son. So, better than anyone in the universe, God empathized with Randy's pain.

A lot of bad theology inevitably surfaces when we face suffering. When people lose their faith because of suffering, it suggests a weak or nominal faith that didn't account for or prepare them for evil and suffering. Any faith not based on the truth needs to be lost—the sooner, the better.

Suffering and evil exert a force that either pushes us away from God or pulls us toward him. But if personal suffering gives sufficient evidence that God doesn't exist, then surely I shouldn't wait until *I* suffer to conclude he's a myth. If my suffering would one day justify denying God, then I should deny him now in light of other people's suffering.

Believing that God exists is not the same as *trusting* the God who exists. A nominal Christian often discovers in suffering that his faith has been in his church, family, career, or social network, but not Christ. As he faces evil and suffering, he may find his beliefs shaken or even destroyed. But genuine faith—trusting God even when we don't understand—will be made stronger and purer.

If your faith is based on lack of affliction, it's on the brink of extinction and is only a frightening diagnosis or a shattering phone call away from collapse. Token faith will not survive suffering. Nor should it.

Thank you, Lord, for welcoming the honest cries of our hearts. Thank you for allowing us to ask, "Why?" It's a gift to us that your prophets and King David asked, "Why," and even your Son, Jesus, asked, "Why?" as he hung on a cross. But give us the grace and wisdom, Lord, to ask our questions while looking to your Word and to your Holy Spirit for answers.

Sorrow's End

Then I saw a new heaven and a new earth, for the first heaven and the first earth had passed away, and there was no longer any sea. I saw the Holy City, the new Jerusalem, coming down out of heaven from God, prepared as a bride beautifully dressed for her husband. And I heard a loud voice from the throne saying, "Now the dwelling of God is with men, and he will live with them. They will be his people, and God himself will be with them and be their God. He will wipe every tear from their eyes. There will be no more death or mourning or crying or pain, for the old order of things has passed away."

He who was seated on the throne said, "I am making everything new!" Then he said, "Write this down, for these words are trustworthy and true."

—REVELATION 21:1–5

God promises that one day there will be no more death or mourning or crying or pain. As we are acutely aware, that day has not yet come. But notice how Jesus caps off his promise to his disciple John: he says John should write the words down because they are "trustworthy and true." In other words, he is saying, "John, my beloved friend and servant, you can take these words to the bank; I'll stake my life on them. In fact, I already have."

Christ promises—in writing—a resurrected life on the New Earth, an eternal life without sorrow and pain in a glorious new world. Talk about light at the end of the tunnel!

Our own suffering is often our wake-up call to the world's suffering. But even if you aren't now facing it, look around and you'll see many who are. If we open our eyes, we'll see the problem of evil and suffering even when it doesn't touch us directly.

The loss of American lives in the terrorist attacks of September 11, 2001, numbered 2,973—horrible indeed, yet a small fraction of the terror and loss of life faced daily around the world. The death toll in the 1994 Rwandan genocide, for example, amounted to more than *two* World Trade Center disasters *every day for one hundred days straight*. Americans discovered in one day what much of the world already knew—violent death comes quickly, hits hard, and can be unspeakably appalling.

Yet no suffering is like our own suffering. After his wife died, a grief-torn C. S. Lewis realized, "If I had really cared, as I thought I did, about the sorrows of the world, I should not have been so overwhelmed when my own sorrow came."[2]

Sufferers have told me, "We did everything right. We attended church and gave our money to missions—and then God did this to us. I don't get it." At times like these our faith gets exposed as an insurance policy for which our good behavior is the premium we pay to protect us from harm.

Devastation and tragedy feel just as real for those with faith as they do for those who have none. But knowledge that others have suffered and learned to trust God anyway gives the faithful strength to keep going. Because they do not place their hope for health and abundance and secure relationships in this life but in an eternal life to come, believers' hope remains firm regardless of what happens.

And on the other side of death, God promises that all who know him will experience acceptance into his holy, loving, and gracious arms—which is the greatest miracle, the answer to the problem of evil and suffering. He promises us an eternal kingdom on the New Earth, where he will wipe away every tear from the eyes of those who come to trust him in this present and temporary world of pain.

Lord, thank you for your promise of a new and glorious and everlasting life on a redeemed Earth, with you and all of my spiritual family. Help me to trust you today, to sense your arms around me and your gentle hands even now beginning to wipe away my tears.

6

Suffering Is No Accident

Come, O children, listen to me;
    I will teach you the fear of the LORD.
What man is there who desires life
    and loves many days, that he may see good?
Keep your tongue from evil
    and your lips from speaking deceit.
Turn away from evil and do good;
    seek peace and pursue it.
The eyes of the LORD are toward the righteous
    and his ears toward their cry.
The face of the LORD is against those who do evil,
    to cut off the memory of them from the earth.
When the righteous cry for help, the LORD hears
    and delivers them out of all their troubles.
The LORD is near to the brokenhearted
    and saves the crushed in spirit.
Many are the afflictions of the righteous,
    but the LORD delivers him out of them all.

—PSALM 34:11–19, ESV

M any believe that suffering is never God's will. But this Scripture tells us that it often *is*. And these verses affirm God's faithfulness even as we suffer.

A young woman battling cancer wrote me, "I was surprised that when it happened, it was hard and it hurt and I was sad and I couldn't find anything good or redeeming about my losses. I never expected that a Christian who had access to God could feel so empty and alone."

Unfortunately, most of us don't give focused thought to evil and suffering until we experience them. This forces us to formulate perspective on the fly, at a time when our thinking is muddled and we're exhausted and consumed by pressing issues. If you've been there, you'll attest to the fact that it's far better to think through suffering in advance.

Pastor James Montgomery Boice had a clear perspective. In May 2000, he stood before his Philadelphia church and explained that he'd been diagnosed with liver cancer:

Should you pray for a miracle? Well, you're free to do that, of course. My general impression is that the God who is able to do miracles—and He certainly can—is also able to keep you from getting the problem in the first place. So although miracles do happen, they're rare by definition.... Above all, I would say pray for the glory of God. If you think of God glorifying Himself in history and you say, where in all of history has God most glorified Himself? He did it at the cross of Jesus Christ, and it wasn't by delivering Jesus from the cross, though He could have....

God is in charge. When things like this come into our lives, they are not accidental. It's not as if God somehow forgot what was going on, and something bad slipped by.... God is not only the one who is in charge; God is also good. Everything He does is good.... If God does something in your life, would you change it? If you'd change it, you'd make it worse. It wouldn't be as good.[3]

Eight weeks later, having taught his people first how to live and then how to die, Pastor Boice departed this world to "be with Christ, which is better by far" (Philippians 1:23).

Suffering will come; we owe it to God, ourselves, and those around us to prepare for it.

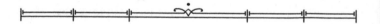

Lord, as I and those I love face hardship and suffering, give me that same sense of your grace and purpose that Pastor Boice enjoyed. Remind me that for those who bow their knees to you in repentance and faith, our present suffering will be replaced by the eternal pleasures of your presence, where joy will be the air we breathe.

7

Cultivating Christlikeness

His divine power has given us everything we need for life and godliness through our knowledge of him who called us by his own glory and goodness. Through these he has given us his very great and precious promises, so that through them you may participate in the divine nature and escape the corruption in the world caused by evil desires.

For this very reason, make every effort to add to your faith goodness; and to goodness, knowledge; and to knowledge, self-control; and to self-control, perseverance; and to perseverance, godliness; and to godliness, brotherly kindness; and to brotherly kindness, love. For if you possess these qualities in increasing measure, they will keep you from being ineffective and unproductive in your knowledge of our Lord Jesus Christ....

For if you do these things, you will never fall, and you will receive a rich welcome into the eternal kingdom of our Lord and Savior Jesus Christ.

—2 PETER 1:3–8, 10–11

us by his own glory and goodness and given us
nises to help generate his character qualities in our
difficulties, he is at work to make us productive
the fruit of his Spirit.

Christian home, Jeremy was bitter toward God be-
rents had been born with cerebral palsy. He broke his
en, as a young man, Jeremy told him he would never
who had done this to his parents.

fe became a train wreck of drugs and alcohol. He went
ilitation centers and two separations from his wife, who
y-seven years for her husband to trust Christ.

d for drunk driving, Jeremy finally broke. He yielded his
and immediately felt the bitterness lift.

early three decades of pain in her marriage, Jeremy's wife,
te, "I am here to tell you I would not have the relationship
that I have if I had not suffered deeply. God revealed trea-
me that can only be found, I believe, in the darkness."

ah comes to the problem of evil from a distinct worldview. But
e other views. Each attempts to answer the question, "How
reconcile evil and suffering with a God who is all-good, all-
ful, and all-knowing?" Besides the irrational conclusion that
d suffering must not exist and the atheistic conclusion that God
not exist, the most popular ways of addressing the problem of
ninimize one or more of God's attributes, especially his power,
wledge, or goodness.

A friend wrestled with the problem of evil after a terrible accident.
concluded that we err whenever we speak of only two or three
ributes of God in relation to the problem of evil. He meant that we

must bring *all* of God's attributes to the table. To merely glorify and magnify God is not to make more of him than he is; that's impossible. But to stop there is to do injustice to his infinite majesty, power, wisdom, and love.

If we see God *only* in terms of his love or mercy or compassion—as wonderful as those attributes are—we will not worship the true God but an idol of our own imagination. An idol that will, in the end, disappoint us, just as everything that is not God always will.

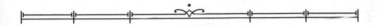

God, give us wisdom to see the world through your eyes. As you showed your servant Sarah, Jeremy's wife, show us that in our suffering you can accomplish the grand purpose of cultivating in us Christlike qualities of faith, kindness, perseverance, love, and goodness in increasing measure. Help us anticipate the rich welcome you will grant those who have submitted to your purposes to prepare us for the Person and Place we most desire.

Filling Faith's Reservoir

David praised the LORD in the presence of the whole assembly, saying,
"Praise be to you, O LORD,

God of our father Israel,

from everlasting to everlasting.

Yours, O LORD, is the greatness and the power

and the glory and the majesty and the splendor,

for everything in heaven and earth is yours.

Yours, O LORD, is the kingdom;

you are exalted as head over all.

Wealth and honor come from you;

you are the ruler of all things.

In your hands are strength and power

to exalt and give strength to all.

Now, our God, we give you thanks,

and praise your glorious name.

—1 CHRONICLES 29:10–13

God is the cosmic center, the source, and the reference point from which all else, including every aspect of our lives, derives its meaning. Gratitude, thanksgiving, and praise are the natural responses of our hearts when we recognize that God is what the universe is all about and that there is no purpose higher than his glory.

To address good and evil without gazing upon God is fruitless. Good flows from the life connected to God.

"Anyone who does what is good is from God. Anyone who does what is evil has not seen God" (3 John 11). To embrace good and turn from evil, we must see God *as he really is*. We must not simply believe *in* God but believe what is true *about* God. When we see God as he is, we will see ourselves as we are, leaving him in his rightful place and putting us in ours.

Darrell Scott's daughter Rachel was the first to die in 1999's Columbine school shootings. I asked Darrell what we should do to prepare for evil and suffering. Without hesitation he answered, "Become a student of God's Word."

Darrell's view of God already had a firm place in his heart when Rachel died. He trusted from the first that God had a purpose. While this did not remove his pain, it did provide solid footing from which he could move forward, trusting God instead of resenting him.

In my experience, most Christians lack grounding in God's attributes, including his sovereignty, omnipotence, omniscience, justice, and patience. We dare not wait for the time of crisis to learn perspective! "Don't be content to be hand-fed by others," Darrell said. "Do your own reading and study; devour good books; talk about the things of God."

Before I became a scuba diver, I learned in a classroom how to use the equipment. My friend Don Maxwell and I studied and discussed the manual at length. Obviously, the underwater world differed considerably from the classroom and Don's living room. But what we learned outside the water gave us a great head start in coping with real-life underwater challenges.

Studying about evil and suffering doesn't equal facing it, but it can go a long way in preparing us for it, provided we see it in relationship to both the goodness and greatness of God. This will provide a reservoir of perspective from which we can draw. It will minimize disorientation and panic when we plunge into life's turbulence. This is why I encourage you to meditate on and discuss with others the themes addressed in this book.

We shouldn't wait until suffering comes to start learning how to face it any more than we should wait until we fall into deep water to start learning how to scuba dive.

God, help us to prepare for suffering by seeing you as the center of gravity for the entire cosmos. Help us break out of the gravitational pull of our own small lives and forever abandon the illusion that the world should revolve around us. Remind us through our sufferings and failures that we dare not trust in ourselves but only in you and your sovereign grace.

Renewed Through Worship

We are hard pressed on every side, but not crushed; perplexed, but not in despair; persecuted, but not abandoned; struck down, but not destroyed. We always carry around in our body the death of Jesus, so that the life of Jesus may also be revealed in our body. For we who are alive are always being given over to death for Jesus' sake, so that his life may be revealed in our mortal body. So then, death is at work in us, but life is at work in you.

It is written: "I believed; therefore I have spoken." With that same spirit of faith we also believe and therefore speak, because we know that the one who raised the Lord Jesus from the dead will also raise us with Jesus and present us with you in his presence. All this is for your benefit, so that the grace that is reaching more and more people may cause thanksgiving to overflow to the glory of God.

Therefore we do not lose heart. Though outwardly we are wasting away, yet inwardly we are being renewed day by day. For our light and momentary troubles are achieving for us an eternal glory that far outweighs them all. So we fix our eyes not on what is seen, but on what is unseen. For what is seen is temporary, but what is unseen is eternal.

—2 CORINTHIANS 4:8–18

Hard pressed, but not crushed; perplexed, but not in despair; persecuted, but not abandoned; struck down, but not destroyed? Anyone who thinks the Bible doesn't face suffering head-on hasn't read it. Yet, while outwardly wasting away, those who draw on Christ within, who listen to God's Holy Spirit speak to them through his Word, and who gather with the church, Christ's body, can be renewed day after day.

Robert Rogers's entire family drowned in a 2003 Kansas flash flood. In a moment, he lost his beloved wife and all four of his children. This Christ-centered family went to church, tithed, read the Bible, and prayed together. After the disaster, Robert entered a dark world of Job-like suffering.

We need only to read Scripture, or look around us, or live long enough in order to learn that *trusting God doesn't ward off all evil and suffering.* He never said it would. In fact, he said just the opposite… but with a promise: "In this world you will have trouble. But take heart! I have overcome the world" (John 16:33).

On the worst day of his life, his ten children taken from him, Job worshiped God. On the worst day of his life, when a flood swept away his wife and four children, Robert Rogers turned to God in worship. He told me he did so because he felt his loss so deeply that he could not lose the one object he had left to grab on to: God. He couldn't function, couldn't go on living, without worshiping God.

Believers share common ground with unbelievers. We feel mutual horror at the reality, depth, and duration of human and animal suffering. We share a conviction that this kind of pain is terribly wrong and that it should be made right.

Consider what Paul wrote:

> Our present sufferings are not worth comparing with the
> glory that will be revealed in us. (Romans 8:18)

"Well," a critic might say, "such affirmations reflect the naive idealism of someone insulated from evil and suffering." But the apostle Paul made these statements. He'd suffered through hunger, thirst, cold, imprisonment, murderous mob attacks, and repeated beatings and floggings—five times within an inch of his life. He described himself as "exposed to death again and again." *This* is what Paul means by "our present sufferings" and "our light and momentary troubles."

Paul insists that our sufferings will result in our greater good— God's people will be better off *eternally* because they suffer *temporarily*. From Paul's perspective, this trade-off will in eternity prove to be a great bargain.

In fact, the argument for the *greater good* may be the strongest biblical case for God's permitting evil and suffering. However, this requires trust on our part, since the promised greater good is future and we can't see it in the present. Faith is called for, since we do not know everything God knows. But instead of trusting ourselves and our flawed judgment, we can choose to trust the one who has an eternal plan of sovereign grace and has gone to inconceivable lengths to see that it will be accomplished.

Lord, you tell us that though it may seem heavy, compared to eternal glory, our current suffering is light and momentary. You tell us not to fix our eyes on popular culture, not on fleeting accomplishments and wealth, but upon what is eternal, what will still matter a billion years from now. Remind us to focus on you, our soon-returning Savior, instead of on our suffering. Give us the eyes of faith. Don't wait until tomorrow, Lord, for we need faith today, this very moment.

A Lion on God's Leash

As for you, you were dead in your transgressions and sins, in which you used to live when you followed the ways of this world and of the ruler of the kingdom of the air, the spirit who is now at work in those who are disobedient. All of us also lived among them at one time, gratifying the cravings of our sinful nature and following its desires and thoughts. Like the rest, we were by nature objects of wrath. But because of his great love for us, God, who is rich in mercy, made us alive with Christ even when we were dead in transgressions—it is by grace you have been saved. And God raised us up with Christ and seated us with him in the heavenly realms in Christ Jesus, in order that in the coming ages he might show the incomparable riches of his grace, expressed in his kindness to us in Christ Jesus.

— EPHESIANS 2:1–7

I n a radical work of supernatural transformation, God has, in Christ, made alive his children who were once spiritually dead slaves of sin. By his grace he has saved us from the devil and his fallen angels and given us a fixed position in Christ's kingdom in Heaven.

What's the opposite of light? Darkness. What's the opposite of good? Evil. When asked to name the opposite of God, people often answer, "Satan." But that's false. Michael, the righteous archangel, is Satan's opposite. Satan is finite; God is infinite. God has no equal. The cosmic clash between God and Satan resembles the undefeated world heavyweight champion (God) taking on a cranky three-year-old (Satan).

Satan and God do not engage in hand-to-hand combat, with Satan sometimes getting the edge. That's not the Bible; that's *Star Wars*.

Satan is called the "god of this world" (2 Corinthians 4:4, ESV), "the prince of the power of the air" (Ephesians 2:2, ESV), and one of the "cosmic powers over this present darkness" (Ephesians 6:12, ESV). But Scripture always describes Satan's power in the context of God's absolute sovereignty. Satan remains under God's authority at all times. The devil is nowhere close to being omnipotent, omniscient, omnipresent, or in any other way on God's level.

Satan inflicts evil and suffering on both the world and God's people. He is "like a roaring lion, seeking someone to devour" (1 Peter 5:8, NASB). That describes only part of the picture, however. Satan is a lion, yes, but a lion on God's leash.

Knowing the infinite difference between the power of Satan and the power of God, Charles Spurgeon said, "It would be a very sharp and trying experience to me to think that I have an affliction which God never sent me, that the bitter cup was never filled by his hand, that my trials were never measured out by him, nor sent to me by his arrangement of their weight and quantity."[4]

Though Satan seeks to devour us, he poses no threat to God. We are no match for Satan, yet we're told, "Submit yourselves, then, to God. Resist the devil, and he will flee from you" (James 4:7). We should never quote the last part of that verse without the first: *submit yourselves to God.* That alone is the basis upon which we can successfully resist the devil.

When Christ commands, the devil himself obeys. Then the question is, "Why doesn't God once and for all command the devil to stop inflicting evil and suffering on human beings God loves?"

While God assures us that he will one day remove all suffering and sorrow, he will do so only when it accomplishes his greatest glory, which is also our greatest good: "The LORD will be your everlasting light, and your God will be your glory" (Isaiah 60:19). If we come to see the purpose of the universe as God's long-term glory rather than our short-term happiness, then we will undergo a critical paradigm shift in tackling the problem of evil and suffering.

The world has gone terribly wrong.

God is going to fix it.

First, for his eternal glory.

Second, for our eternal good.

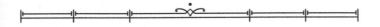

Father, thank you for the promise of deliverance and for your purpose and plan in which our salvation, purchased in Christ, will be fully and completely and finally realized. Help us anticipate the glorious fulfillment of your great promise that in the coming ages you will continuously reveal

*to us the incomparable riches of your grace, expressed in
your kindness to us in Christ Jesus. And until then, even
today, give us glimpses of that grace and kindness for which
we owe you all gratitude and praise.*

II

Wretched Sinner, Gracious God

I thank Christ Jesus our Lord, who has given me strength, that he considered me faithful, appointing me to his service. Even though I was once a blasphemer and a persecutor and a violent man, I was shown mercy because I acted in ignorance and unbelief. The grace of our Lord was poured out on me abundantly, along with the faith and love that are in Christ Jesus.

Here is a trustworthy saying that deserves full acceptance: Christ Jesus came into the world to save sinners—of whom I am the worst. But for that very reason I was shown mercy so that in me, the worst of sinners, Christ Jesus might display his unlimited patience as an example for those who would believe on him and receive eternal life. Now to the King eternal, immortal, invisible, the only God, be honor and glory for ever and ever. Amen.

—1 Timothy 1:12–17

In 1750, at age twenty-five, John Newton commanded an English slave ship. He anchored off the African coast, purchasing natives taken captive by rival tribes. The slave traders took the terrified slaves aboard and chained them belowdecks in two-foot-high pens to prevent suicides. As many as six hundred lay side by side like fireplace logs, row after row. There were no toilet facilities or ventilation. The stench was indescribable. Sometimes a quarter of the slaves died on the journey.

As a young crewman, when his ship nearly sank, Newton professed Christ. But he prided himself on being incorrigible. He spent years committing evil before he experienced a true conversion. He left the slave trade and felt increasing remorse for what he'd done.

At age eighty-two, shortly before his death, a physically blind but spiritually sighted John Newton said, "My memory is nearly gone, but I remember two things: That I am a great sinner, and that Christ is a great Saviour."[5]

Newton's tombstone reads, "John Newton...once an infidel... was, by the rich mercy of our Lord and Saviour Jesus Christ, preserved, restored, pardoned, and appointed to preach the faith he had long labored to destroy."

Newton wrote hundreds of hymns, the most famous of which is the most popular song among many Christians in Africa and throughout the world:

Amazing grace! How sweet the sound
that saved a wretch like me!

The clearest indication of the depth of our evil is what it cost to redeem us. We need not be perfect to please God in this life, but we must believe in Jesus' ability to rescue us—to achieve for us the moral perfection required so we may live forever with God.

Newton's claim to wretchedness wasn't hyperbole; he clearly saw the evil in himself, an evil that many are more successful at hiding. While Newton may appear an extreme case, the Bible teaches that all of us are evil-lovers and evildoers, blind wretches in desperate need of God's transforming grace.

I thank God for the connectedness of humanity that allowed not just the first Adam to introduce evil and suffering to the human race, but the last Adam, Jesus Christ, to take that evil and suffering on himself.

Lord, the apostle Paul, who persecuted Christians, called himself the worst of sinners. John Newton thought the same of himself. May we see ourselves as the worst of sinners, with our sins bigger in our eyes than the sins of others (yet never too big for you to forgive). Thank you for choosing us, unworthy though we are, that Christ Jesus might display his unlimited patience as an example for others around us. May our humble acknowledgment of our unworthiness and your great grace draw others to believe in you and to accept your gift of eternal life.

12

What Makes Grace So Amazing

You see, at just the right time, when we were still powerless, Christ died for the ungodly. Very rarely will anyone die for a righteous man, though for a good man someone might possibly dare to die. But God demonstrates his own love for us in this: While we were still sinners, Christ died for us.

Since we have now been justified by his blood, how much more shall we be saved from God's wrath through him! For if, when we were God's enemies, we were reconciled to him through the death of his Son, how much more, having been reconciled, shall we be saved through his life!

—ROMANS 5:6–10

A woman with a wonderful voice sang one of my favorite songs, "Amazing Grace," just before I spoke at a gathering. It sounded beautiful, until she got to the tenth word: "Amazing grace! How sweet the sound that saved a *soul* like me!"

My heart sank. The word *wretch* had vanished, replaced by the more positive word *soul*. Can you imagine what John Newton, the composer and former slave trader, might have said? Newton recognized himself as a wretch—and that's what made God's grace so "amazing." The greater our grasp of our sin and alienation from God, the greater our grasp of God's amazing grace.

The Bible says, "While we were still sinners, Christ died for us" (Romans 5:8). If we don't allow the word *sinners* its actual meaning, we miss the point. When we cut *wretch* out of "Amazing Grace," we reduce it to something more sensible, less surprising. If we weren't so bad without Christ, then why did he have to endure the Cross? Paul said if men were good enough without Jesus, then "Christ died for nothing" (Galatians 2:21).

Charles Spurgeon put it this way: "Too many think lightly of sin, and therefore think lightly of the Saviour."[6] We try to explain away sin in terms of a "bad day" or "that's not what I meant" or "I did what my father always did to me" or "I wouldn't have done this if you hadn't done that." All these statements minimize our evil and thereby *minimize the greatness of God's grace in atoning for our evil.*

Grace isn't about God lowering his standards. It's about God fulfilling those standards through the substitutionary suffering of Jesus Christ. Grace never ignores or violates truth. Grace gave what truth demanded: the ultimate sacrifice for our wickedness.

God's grace is greater than my sin. But my ability to measure the greatness of his grace depends upon my willingness, in brokenness before him, to recognize the greatness of my sin. "God opposes the proud but gives grace to the humble" (1 Peter 5:5). The proud deny their evil; the humble confess it.

A profound awareness of my evil should move my heart to praise God for the wonders of his grace.

Father, what a remarkable promise to us that, unworthy as we are, if we ask, we'll receive; if we seek, we'll find; if we knock, the door will be opened. We've learned the hard way that this doesn't always mean we'll get what we want. But it does mean we'll get what you know to be ultimately best for us. The gate is small and the road is narrow, so please guide us and keep us on the path of righteousness, for your glory.

13

Safe in Our Father's Arms

After Jesus said this, he looked toward heaven and prayed: "Father, the time has come. Glorify your Son, that your Son may glorify you. For you granted him authority over all people that he might give eternal life to all those you have given him. Now this is eternal life: that they may know you, the only true God, and Jesus Christ, whom you have sent. I have brought you glory on earth by completing the work you gave me to do. And now, Father, glorify me in your presence with the glory I had with you before the world began....

"I pray for them. I am not praying for the world, but for those you have given me, for they are yours.... Holy Father, protect them by the power of your name—the name you gave me—so that they may be one as we are one. While I was with them, I protected them and kept them safe by that name you gave me.... My prayer is not that you take them out of the world but that you protect them from the evil one. They are not of the world, even as I am not of it. Sanctify them by the truth; your word is truth. As you sent me into the world, I have sent them into the world. For them I sanctify myself, that they too may be truly sanctified.

"My prayer is not for them alone. I pray also for those who will believe in me through their message, that all of them may be one, Father, just as you are in me and I am in you. May they also be in us so that the world may believe that you have sent me."

—JOHN 17:1–5, 9, 11–12, 15–21

Doesn't it touch you to realize that two thousand years ago Jesus was praying for you? He praised the Father for the eternal life given to his children and prayed for our protection from Satan.

Protecting his children is what a father does. In 1988, an Armenian earthquake killed forty-five thousand. In the chaos, one man made his way to his son's school only to find nothing but rubble. Other parents stumbled around dazed and weeping, calling out their children's names. But this father ran to the back corner of the building where his son's classroom had been, and began digging.

To everyone else, it seemed hopeless. How could his son have survived? But this father had promised he would always be there for his boy, so he heaved rocks and dug, calling for his son by name: "Armand!"

Well-meaning parents and bystanders tried to pull him away from the rubble. "It's too late!" "They're dead!" "There's nothing you can do!" The fire chief tried to dissuade him, saying, "Fires and explosions are happening everywhere. You're in danger. Go home!" Finally, the police came and said, "You're in shock. You're endangering others. Go home. We'll handle it!"

But the man continued to dig, hour after hour—eight hours, then twelve, twenty-four, thirty-six hours. Finally, in the thirty-eighth hour of digging—a day and a half after everyone told him to give up hope—he called his son's name again, pulled back a big rock, and heard his son's voice.

"Armand!" the father screamed.

From under the rocks came the words, "Dad? I told them! I told the other kids that if you were still alive, you'd save me!"

The father helped his son and thirteen other children climb out of the rubble. When the building had collapsed, the children survived in a tentlike pocket. The father lovingly carried his son home to his mother. When the townspeople praised Armand's father for saving the children, he simply explained, "I promised my son, 'No matter what, I'll be there for you!'"[7]

So it is with God our Father and his love shown to us in Jesus.

Lord Jesus, thank you for praying for us. Father, thank you for answering Jesus' prayers. Thank you for your persistent love. Thank you for never giving up on your children, as Armand's father refused to give up on finding his son. Thank you for paying the price to find us. May we be willing to pay a great price to search the world's rubble and uncover others for whom you shed your blood.

14

Our Refuge and Strength

Keep me safe, O God,
> for in you I take refuge.
I said to the Lord, "You are my Lord;
> apart from you I have no good thing."...
Lord, you have assigned me my portion and my cup;
> you have made my lot secure.
The boundary lines have fallen for me in pleasant places;
> surely I have a delightful inheritance.
I will praise the Lord, who counsels me;
> even at night my heart instructs me.
I have set the Lord always before me.
> Because he is at my right hand,
> I will not be shaken.
Therefore my heart is glad and my tongue rejoices;
> my body also will rest secure,
because you will not abandon me to the grave,
> nor will you let your Holy One see decay.
You have made known to me the path of life;
> you will fill me with joy in your presence,
> with eternal pleasures at your right hand.

—Psalm 16:1–2, 5–11

God is the source of all good things. He is our refuge. Those who recognize his presence and call upon him, those who live with a daily awareness of the eternal pleasures he has promised us, those who set the Lord always before them, in the end will not be shaken.

An unskilled truck driver who obtained his license through bribery allowed a large object to fall from his truck onto a Milwaukee freeway in front of Scott and Janet Willis's van. Their gas tank exploded, killing six of their children.

Standing before cameras and microphones, Scott Willis said:

> The depth of our pain is indescribable. However, the Bible expresses our feelings that we sorrow, but not as those without hope. What gives us our firm foundation for hope are the words of God found in Scripture.… Ben, Joe, Sam, Hank, Elizabeth and Peter are all with Jesus Christ. We know where they are. Our strength rests in God's Word.[8]

Fourteen years after the tragic event, Janet told me, "Today I have a far greater understanding of the goodness of God than I did before the accident." This might have taken my breath away had I not already heard it from others who've also endured unspeakable suffering. At the end of our two-hour conversation, Scott Willis stated, "I have a stronger view of God's sovereignty than ever before."

Scott and Janet did not say that the accident itself strengthened their view of God's sovereignty. Indeed, Scott's overwhelming sense of loss initially prompted suicidal thoughts. Rather, their faith grew as they threw themselves upon God for grace to live each day. "I turned to God for strength," Janet said, "because I had no strength." She went to the Bible with a hunger for God's presence, and he met her. "I learned about him. He made sense when nothing else made sense. If it weren't for the Lord, I would have lost my sanity."

Is that denial? Is it wishful thinking? Or is it the real power and transforming grace of God that came in suffering? I'm convinced it was God's grace.

I asked Scott and Janet, "What would you say to those who reject the Christian faith because they think that no plan of God—nothing at all—could possibly be worth the suffering of your children and your suffering over all these years?"

"Eternity is a long time," Janet replied. "It will be worth it. Our children's suffering was brief, and they have the eternal joy of being with God. We and their grandparents have suffered since. But our suffering has been small compared to our children's joy. Fourteen years is a short time compared to eternity. We'll be with them there, forever."

La Rochefoucauld may have best captured the difference between one person's lost faith and another's deepened faith in the face of suffering: "A great storm puts out a little fire, but it feeds a strong one."

Lord, may we set you always before us by daily meditating on your Word and praying to you as the day unfolds. May we present our petitions boldly before your throne and sit quietly at your feet as we await your response. We will die, but you will not abandon us to the grave. Comfort us with the knowledge that family members and friends covered by

Christ's blood are not lost to us, because we know where they are, and we await the great reunion. Like Scott and Janet Willis, may we cling to your promise of resurrection. Fill us with joy in your presence, helping us to envision the eternal pleasures at your right hand.

15

God's Good Gifts

Give thanks to the LORD, call on his name;
    make known among the nations what he has done.
Sing to him, sing praise to him;
    tell of all his wonderful acts.
Glory in his holy name;
    let the hearts of those who seek the LORD rejoice.
Look to the LORD and his strength;
    seek his face always.
Remember the wonders he has done,
    his miracles, and the judgments he pronounced,
O descendants of Israel his servant,
    O sons of Jacob, his chosen ones.
He is the LORD our God;
    his judgments are in all the earth.
He remembers his covenant forever,
    the word he commanded, for a thousand generations....
Sing to the LORD, all the earth;
    proclaim his salvation day after day.
Declare his glory among the nations,
    his marvelous deeds among all peoples.

For great is the LORD and most worthy of praise;
　　he is to be feared above all gods....
Let the heavens rejoice, let the earth be glad;
　　let them say among the nations, "The LORD reigns!"
Let the sea resound, and all that is in it;
　　let the fields be jubilant, and everything in them!
Then the trees of the forest will sing,
　　they will sing for joy before the LORD,
　　for he comes to judge the earth.
Give thanks to the LORD, for he is good;
　　his love endures forever.
Cry out, "Save us, O God our Savior;
　　gather us and deliver us from the nations,
that we may give thanks to your holy name,
　　that we may glory in your praise."
Praise be to the LORD, the God of Israel,
　　from everlasting to everlasting.
Then all the people said "Amen" and "Praise the LORD."
　　　　—1 CHRONICLES 16:8–15, 23–25, 31–36

Reasons to give thanks to God are unending. They come in all sizes. By God's Spirit, through his Word, and by observing the world around us, we may cultivate the vision to see a thousand things each day that prompt our hearts to praise him.

Much of the good of this world, such as the beauty of a flower or the grandeur of a waterfall or the joy of an otter at play, serves no more practical purpose than great art. It does, however, serve the high purpose of filling us with delight, wonder, and gratitude.

Thomas Schmidt tells of an old woman he met in a nursing home. Blind and almost deaf, Mabel was eighty-nine. She'd lived there for twenty-five years and now sat strapped in a wheelchair.

Schmidt handed Mabel a flower and said, "Happy Mother's Day."

She tried to smell it. "Thank you," she said, her words garbled. "It's lovely. But since I'm blind, can I give it to someone else?" When he wheeled her to another resident, she held out the flower and said, "Here, this is from Jesus."

Schmidt asked, "Mabel, what do you think about when you lie in your room?"

"I think about my Jesus."

"What do you think about Jesus?"

As she spoke slowly and deliberately, he wrote down her words: "I think how good he's been to me. He's been awfully good.… I'm one of those kind who's mostly satisfied.… I'd rather have Jesus. He's all the world to me."[9]

Why does anyone feel gratitude? And why do people, even irreligious survivors of a plane crash, so often thank God? Do people thank time, chance, and natural selection for the good they experience? No, because innately we see life as a gift from God.

Some of the world's goodness can be described only as supernatural since from a naturalistic viewpoint we should all ruthlessly step on one another to survive. Despite its current flaws, the world's beauty and goodness testify to a Creator who designed it with order and purpose. Don't evil and suffering grab our attention precisely because they are *not* the norm in our lives? Our shock at evil testifies to the predominance of good.

The Christian worldview explains goodness as rooted in God, revealed by God, and rewarded by him. It gives reason for great optimism to those who embrace it.

Lord, help us to see the goodness around us: faithful people, food, dogs and waterfalls, sports and the arts, and the very air we breathe. Thank you for all that comes from you, for you are the source of all good things. Thank you for preparing a place for us of eternal goodness and natural wonders that will unmistakably shout your greatness and kindness for all to see.

16

God's Infinite Power

I keep asking that the God of our Lord Jesus Christ, the glorious Father, may give you the Spirit of wisdom and revelation, so that you may know him better. I pray also that the eyes of your heart may be enlightened in order that you may know the hope to which he has called you, the riches of his glorious inheritance in the saints, and his incomparably great power for us who believe. That power is like the working of his mighty strength, which he exerted in Christ when he raised him from the dead and seated him at his right hand in the heavenly realms, far above all rule and authority, power and dominion, and every title that can be given, not only in the present age but also in the one to come. And God placed all things under his feet and appointed him to be head over everything for the church, which is his body, the fullness of him who fills everything in every way.

—Ephesians 1:17–23

Paul's persistent prayer is that his people may know Christ better and realize "his incomparably great power for us who believe." His attributes of "mighty strength" and his rule and authority and dominion over all assure us that he can and will keep all his promises.

In *When Bad Things Happen to Good People,* Rabbi Harold Kushner wrote that he believes some things are "too difficult even for God." He said, "I can worship a God who hates suffering but cannot eliminate it, more easily than I can worship a God who chooses to make children suffer and die, for whatever exalted reason."[10]

But a god who can't deliver us *from* suffering cannot deliver us *through* suffering. Chances are, you already have friends who can't control the universe. Do you really need another one, named "God"?

Those who believe in a God of limited power might respond, "It isn't that God can't do anything, just that he can't do everything." Many people might be willing to *try* to rescue my loved ones from a burning building, but I want someone who actually *can.* If God can't prevent our suffering even if he wanted to, then why should we believe he is able to successfully save us in the end?

When asked what allowed her to endure the concentration camp, Corrie ten Boom responded, "Not what, but *Who.*" Then she added, "The devil is strong, but his power is limited; Jesus' power is unlimited."[11]

Jesus sustained Corrie in Ravensbrück. She believed his words: "All authority in heaven and on earth has been given to me" (Matthew 28:18). Suppose instead that Jesus had said to his disciples, "I have a lot of authority, but I'm only in process; human and demonic choices can thwart my limited power. But I sincerely hope things work out for you." How many of his disciples do you think would have willingly died for him?

God compares himself to both father and mother, and if you are his child, he says his care for you is greater than anyone's. He loves you beyond measure and freely offers forgiveness. God is surely loving, but he is also all-powerful. God's omnipotence and love are not in conflict.

Jeremiah 32:17–19 affirms God's love without minimizing his power: "Ah, Sovereign LORD, you have made the heavens and the earth by your great power and outstretched arm. *Nothing is too hard for you. You show love to thousands....* O great and powerful God, whose name is the LORD Almighty, great are your purposes and mighty are your deeds."

Father, help us recognize the infinite vastness of your power so we may see you as you are, not as what finite men would reduce you to. I am grateful that you are in debt to no one and never under anyone's power. Thank you for not merely being mighty but all-mighty, as demonstrated in the creation of the world and the resurrection of Jesus. Because you are all-powerful, nothing can ever keep you from fulfilling each and every one of your great promises to us, your children. Thank you!

17

God's Boundless Knowledge

Praise the LORD.
How good it is to sing praises to our God,
    how pleasant and fitting to praise him!…
He heals the brokenhearted
    and binds up their wounds.
He determines the number of the stars
    and calls them each by name.
Great is our Lord and mighty in power;
    his understanding has no limit.…
The LORD delights in those who fear him,
    who put their hope in his unfailing love.

          —PSALM 147:1, 3–5, 11

God's understanding *has no limit*! God knows everything, including every contingency, and he knows what is ultimately best in ways we cannot. God can see ultimate purposes and plans that we can't see.

We have no way of knowing, for instance, whether a disability might be used to cultivate personal qualities that would more profoundly honor God and bring the person greater eternal reward in Heaven.

Because God knows all things in the past, present, *and* future, God is uniquely qualified to know when to ordain or permit evil and suffering and when not to.

Many years ago, on nine occasions I participated in peaceful, nonviolent civil disobedience—speaking up for the civil rights of unborn children. I briefly went to jail, and abortion clinics brought lawsuits against me and others. It seemed possible that if the lawsuits succeeded, the abortion clinics might take away our house and a good part of our monthly income.

In the several years that we found ourselves in the middle of this stressful situation, Nanci and I would talk with our daughters, assuring them that God remained in control, that he knew everything that would happen, and that we could trust him to use it for good.

Now suppose we had believed in what's called "open theism," that God doesn't know what choices people will make in the future and what will result from those choices. Our conversations with our children would have gone in a remarkably different way: "Girls, we don't know how this lawsuit is going to turn out. We don't know if we'll lose our house. We don't know if you'll be able to continue in school. *And God doesn't know either.* God wishes the best for us, and he'll do what he can to help; but he doesn't have a definite purpose or plan in this, and there's no assurance that this will work out for our good. So don't blame him if the choices of demons, abortion clinic owners, a judge, or a jury ruin our lives. God must respect their free will."

I cannot express how radically different our children's prayers, lives, and peace of mind—as well as our own—would have been had we believed that. Instead, we believed what Scripture teaches, and God helped us trust him and his purpose to work for our ultimate good despite the evil intentions of demons and people. I am eternally grateful for that.

Those who believe that God doesn't know about billions of future choices and the events that flow out of those choices must simply hope for the best. Those who believe in a God who knows "the end from the beginning" (Isaiah 46:10), however, can relax because even though *they* don't know what lies ahead, their sovereign God does.

Father, we take great comfort in realizing that though our own knowledge is remarkably small, yours is infinitely great. There is nothing you do not know. And therefore nothing can take you by surprise; nothing can spoil your plans; nothing can thwart your promises. For that we thank you and praise you!

18

God's Unending Goodness

I will exalt you, my God the King;
    I will praise your name for ever and ever.
Every day I will praise you
    and extol your name for ever and ever.
Great is the LORD and most worthy of praise;
    his greatness no one can fathom.
One generation will commend your works to another;
    they will tell of your mighty acts.
They will speak of the glorious splendor of your majesty,
    and I will meditate on your wonderful works.
They will tell of the power of your awesome works,
    and I will proclaim your great deeds.
They will celebrate your abundant goodness
    and joyfully sing of your righteousness.
The LORD is gracious and compassionate,
    slow to anger and rich in love.
The LORD is good to all;
    he has compassion on all he has made.

—PSALM 145:1–9

God's people celebrate his abundant goodness. Yet in this fallen world, languishing under the Curse, God's goodness is sometimes not apparent. Consider the anguished cry of Jeremiah: "He has driven me away and made me walk in darkness rather than light; indeed, he has turned his hand against me again and again, all day long. He has made my skin and my flesh grow old and has broken my bones. He has besieged me and surrounded me with bitterness and hardship" (Lamentations 3:2–5).

This outcry doesn't appear to affirm God's goodness, does it? It seems remarkable that God would include in his inspired Word such human displays of confusion and frustration.

In *The Lion, the Witch and the Wardrobe,* Susan asks Mr. Beaver if Aslan the Lion is safe. "Who said anything about safe?" Mr. Beaver answers. "'Course he isn't safe. But he's good. He's the King, I tell you."[12]

This is sound theology—God can be good without being safe; he can be loving without bowing to our every wish or desire.

C. S. Lewis points out that kindness "cares not whether its object becomes good or bad, provided only that it escapes suffering."[13] In contrast, love cares for the welfare, not the momentary preferences, of the one loved. This explains why a kind stranger might buy children ice cream, while their parents—who love them far more—might not.

God's goodness entails more than whatever makes us feel warm and happy. We argue that if God were as good as we are, then evil and suffering wouldn't exist. On the contrary, evil and suffering wouldn't exist if we were as good as God is.

My friend David O'Brien told me that God used his cerebral palsy to draw him to dependence on Christ. Is he better off? He's convinced he is. His seventy-five years of suffering are no cosmic accident or satanic victory but a severe mercy from the good hand of God. I haven't met many people more convinced of God's goodness than David O'Brien. He's experienced a lifetime of serious afflictions that many consider senseless evil, but David sees them as tools in the hands of a good God.

Many of us, without realizing it, have walked the Emmaus road (see Luke 24:13–32). Sorrow overwhelms us. Questions plague us. We wonder where God is…when all along he walks beside us.

Father, your Word confirms that although your goodness is sometimes apparent, at other times it is not. Give us faith to cling to the objective reality of your goodness even in the hardest days of our lives. Teach us to bask in your goodness not only for your praise and glory but also to fill a reservoir of realized goodness from which we can draw when our lives seem dry and barren. Remind us always to look ahead to the eternal goodness you have bought us as we look back to the price you paid for us on Good Friday and Resurrection Sunday, when you turned evil on its head to guarantee goodness without end.

19

God's Limitless Love

How great is the love the Father has lavished on us, that we should be called children of God! And that is what we are! The reason the world does not know us is that it did not know him. Dear friends, now we are children of God, and what we will be has not yet been made known. But we know that when he appears, we shall be like him, for we shall see him as he is. Everyone who has this hope in him purifies himself, just as he is pure....

This is how we know what love is: Jesus Christ laid down his life for us. And we ought to lay down our lives for our brothers. If anyone has material possessions and sees his brother in need but has no pity on him, how can the love of God be in him? Dear children, let us not love with words or tongue but with actions and in truth. This then is how we know that we belong to the truth, and how we set our hearts at rest in his presence whenever our hearts condemn us. For God is greater than our hearts, and he knows everything.

—1 JOHN 3:1–3, 16–20

Words are inadequate to express the depths of God's love for us: "How great is the love the Father has lavished on us, that we should be called children of God!" If ever an exclamation point was deserved in a translation, surely it's here!

The apostle John says we know what God's love is because of the unthinkable price Jesus paid for us, to turn us into God's own children, fully acceptable in his sight. God's love *abounds*. It proliferates. It's over-flowing, even excessive—something all sufferers need to hear. But God does not always love us on our preferred terms. C. S. Lewis wrote:

> We want, in fact, not so much a Father in Heaven as a grandfather in heaven...whose plan for the universe was simply that it might be truly said at the end of each day, "a good time was had by all."... I should very much like to live in a universe which was governed on such lines. But since it is abundantly clear that I don't, and since I have reason to believe, nevertheless, that God is Love, I conclude that my conception of love needs correction."[14]

Children who know their father as good and loving experience great security. And the Bible assures us that the God who spun galaxies into being "gathers the lambs in his arms and carries them close to his heart" (Isaiah 40:11).

I heard a story of a kindhearted king who finds a blind, destitute orphan boy while hunting in a forest. He sees that the boy receives the finest of everything. The boy is extremely grateful, and he loves the king, his new father, with all his heart.

When the boy turns twenty, a surgeon performs an operation on his eyes, and for the first time he is able to see. This boy, once a starving orphan, has for some years been a royal prince at home in the king's palace. But something wonderful has happened, something far greater than the magnificent food, gardens, libraries, music, and wonders of the palace. The boy is finally able to *see* the face of the father he adores.

The king's rescue of the destitute child is like our conversion. We initially come to know God's love and enjoy his indwelling presence, but still we cannot fully see. The day is coming, however, when we will live in a glorious world where we *will* fully see and all will be beautiful beyond our imagination.

But all these magnificent wonders will be secondary, mere tributes to the King. For by far our greatest thrill will be when, with resurrected eyes, we see for the first time the face of the God who loved us so much as to pour out his life for us.

John Donne put it beautifully:

I shall rise from the dead…. I shall see the Son of God, the Sun of Glory, and shine myself as that sun shines. I shall be united to the Ancient of Days, to God Himself, who had no morning, never began…. No man ever saw God and lived. And yet, I shall not live till I see God; and when I have seen him, I shall never die.[15]

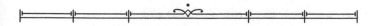

Father, you are the King who found us wandering in our blindness and brought us into your palace. But you did

more than that, for we were not just blind and lost, we were rebels at war against you. Yet in your grace, you gave your Son as a sacrifice to bring us into your family, that we might live with you in security and abundance. How great is your love to have done this for us! And what an unspeakable wonder it will be to behold your face. May we live this day in anticipation of that day!

20

Choosing to Trust

Do not fret because of evil men
    or be envious of those who do wrong;
for like the grass they will soon wither,
    like green plants they will soon die away.
Trust in the LORD and do good;
    dwell in the land and enjoy safe pasture.
Delight yourself in the LORD
    and he will give you the desires of your heart.
Commit your way to the LORD;
    trust in him and he will do this:
He will make your righteousness shine like the dawn,
    the justice of your cause like the noonday sun.
Be still before the LORD and wait patiently for him;
    do not fret when men succeed in their ways,
    when they carry out their wicked schemes.
Refrain from anger and turn from wrath;
    do not fret—it leads only to evil.
For evil men will be cut off,
    but those who hope in the LORD will inherit the land.

A little while, and the wicked will be no more;
>   though you look for them, they will not be found.
But the meek will inherit the land
>   and enjoy great peace.
The wicked plot against the righteous
>   and gnash their teeth at them;
but the Lord laughs at the wicked,
>   for he knows their day is coming.

—PSALM 37:1–13

God calls on us to trust him and to believe that the appearances of current events are very different than the ultimate outcome he has planned and promised. Even when men carry out their wicked schemes, we are to wait patiently for God. The success of evildoers is only apparent and at most temporary. Likewise, the sufferings of God's people will accomplish now-hidden purposes, and those sufferings will be dramatically and forever reversed.

Like Job, we live in a cosmic drama, in full view of Heaven's audience. In the first chapter of Job, the drama's Director tells us what the characters don't know—what's *really* going on. Job knew nothing about God commending him to Satan and calling Job blameless. God let Job face terrible trials with no explanation.

We share this in common with Job—*God doesn't specifically explain why he permits evil and suffering to fall upon us.* He wants us to trust him. In one sense, Job is everyman.

Right now, you and I may be subjects of discussion between God and Satan, just as Job was. Or we may be part of conversations between God and righteous angels, or between angels and redeemed people in Heaven. You may lie in a rest home or a hospital or sit alone in your house. But you're *not* alone—an unseen universe is watching.

You may feel your choices have been reduced to whether you want Jell-O or a window opened or an extra blanket. On the contrary, your choice of whether you will trust God and worship him today reverberates throughout the universe, honoring or dishonoring your God. It also has enormous implications for the eternal rewards God promises us in the next life.

God prepared me to hear the gospel when, as a junior higher, I read fantasy and science fiction stories and gazed at the night sky through my telescope. I'd read of other worlds, of great battles and causes, and I knew that the universe was huge beyond comprehension. I remember the profound loneliness I felt, being on the outside of something so great. Some of the alien worlds I read of captivated me. I believed there *had* to be something better than this world. Without knowing the true story of this universe, I sensed that evil and suffering didn't fit into the story's beginning.

I first read the Bible as a teenager and saw how the world had gone wrong. Three-fourths of the way through the story, I met Jesus and realized he was the One my heart had always longed for. When I got to the end of the story, I saw that God will never give up on this world.

The new world I longed for will be this world reborn. From before the very beginning, God knew the very worst. And he knew how he would turn it into the very best.

Like Job, we look around us and see suffering and evil we do not understand. As Job did in the end, Lord, may we see you now as you truly are, as revealed in your Word, and trust you to accomplish your purposes even when life doesn't make sense to us. Thank you for your sovereign grace in my life, drawing me to yourself even as I grew up in an unbelieving home. I look back now at many difficulties in my life and clearly see your hand. I pray you'll give everyone reading this the ability to see how you have worked in their lives in the past. Give them the faith to see you at work today and the capacity to fully trust you for their future.

21

New Life in
a Redeemed Universe

Then the angel showed me the river of the water of life, as clear as crystal, flowing from the throne of God and of the Lamb down the middle of the great street of the city. On each side of the river stood the tree of life, bearing twelve crops of fruit, yielding its fruit every month. And the leaves of the tree are for the healing of the nations. No longer will there be any curse. The throne of God and of the Lamb will be in the city, and his servants will serve him. They will see his face, and his name will be on their foreheads. There will be no more night. They will not need the light of a lamp or the light of the sun, for the Lord God will give them light. And they will reign for ever and ever. The angel said to me, "These words are trustworthy and true. The Lord, the God of the spirits of the prophets, sent his angel to show his servants the things that must soon take place."

—REVELATION 22:1–6

Think of the world awaiting God's children, redeemed by the blood of Christ. No more Curse. No more suffering. The Tree of Life from the Garden of Eden, a grove of life on both sides of a great freshwater river coming from God's throne. A place where his servants won't be bored but will have things to do, places to go, people to see, all to the glory of Jesus, the King of kings. The New Earth will be filled with natural beauty, offering all the best of our present world with none of the worst!

How long will we need to be in this new home before it will make up for all the suffering we've faced in our lives? Two months? Two weeks? Two days? Two hours? Two minutes?

The bleakest pessimist might answer, "More like a hundred years." But even if you say ten *thousand* years, that will be but the beginning of an eternal life of joy and pleasures at God's right hand (see Psalm 16:11).

What if you could have both complete freedom and complete happiness? Scripture promises exactly that in the New Heaven and New Earth. When we realize God has promised us a redeemed universe and time without end, we'll finally "get it." We'll have opportunity to develop and fulfill dreams bigger than anything we ever had on this fallen Earth.

At the end of Peter Jackson's production of *The Return of the King,* Bilbo Baggins—by then aged and decrepit—gets invited to board an Elven ship bound for Valinor (Heaven). With a smile and a spark of youthful energy in his eyes, he says, "I think I'm quite ready for another adventure."

For the Christian, death is not the end of the adventure but a doorway to a world where dreams and adventures—and relationships—

forever expand. No matter how bad the present, an eternity with Christ in Heaven will completely overshadow it.

Our friends John and Ann Stump watched helplessly as their eighteen-month-old son, Gary, died. Ann said, "In that one moment our life was shattered. My big question was, how could God love me and allow this? If he could have stopped it, why didn't he?"

Nothing could take away the pain, but John and Ann faced a choice concerning their perspective. Ann said, "Even though we still have questions, we've decided to dwell on what we know to be true. I see Heaven in a whole new light. After all, my treasure is there. I look forward to joining him. I can't wait to see him, hug him, hold him, and spend eternity with him."[16]

Instead of dreading the short-term future and further losses it will bring, we can daily look forward to the eternal future, to the joys—including the joys of reunion—that God has promised await us.

Father, thank you for the New Earth that awaits us after the resurrection. Prepare us for our new adventure. Like you did for my friends John and Ann, fill us with anticipation of great reunions with all the redeemed who have gone before us. Remind us, Lord, that we will surely be in your joyous presence only a very short time before realizing that it more than makes up for the worst we ever endured in this old world.

22

Eternal Triumph over Temporary Suffering

My days are swifter than a runner;
>   they fly away without a glimpse of joy.
They skim past like boats of papyrus,
>   like eagles swooping down on their prey.
If I say, "I will forget my complaint,
>   I will change my expression, and smile,"
I still dread all my sufferings,
>   for I know you will not hold me innocent.
Since I am already found guilty,
>   why should I struggle in vain?
Even if I washed myself with soap
>   and my hands with washing soda,
you would plunge me into a slime pit
>   so that even my clothes would detest me.
He is not a man like me that I might answer him,
>   that we might confront each other in court.
If only there were someone to arbitrate between us,
>   to lay his hand upon us both,

someone to remove God's rod from me,
    so that his terror would frighten me no more.
Then I would speak up without fear of him,
    but as it now stands with me, I cannot.

—JOB 9:25–35

I n what may be the oldest book in the Bible, Job complains that because God is not a man, Job cannot go to him about his suffering and expect sympathy or resolution. Job laments, "If only there were someone to arbitrate between us, to lay his hand upon us both, someone to remove God's rod from me."

Who could lay his hand upon both God and man to connect them in loving relationship? Only the God-man, the One who would take God's rod upon himself to pay for the sins of humankind: Jesus.

The Cross is God's answer to the question, "Why don't you do something about evil?" God *did* do something…and what he did was so great and unprecedented that it shook the angelic realm's foundation. It ripped in half, from the top down, not only the temple curtain but the fabric of the universe itself.

What is good about Good Friday? Why isn't it called Bad Friday? Because out of the appallingly bad came what was inexpressibly good. And the good trumps the bad, because though the bad was temporary, the good is eternal.

Evil and suffering formed the crucible in which God demonstrated his love to humankind. His love comes to us soaked in divine blood. One look at Jesus—at his incarnation and the redemption he accomplished for us—should silence the argument that God has withdrawn to some far corner of the universe where he keeps his hands clean and maintains his distance from human suffering.

God does not merely empathize with our sufferings; he actually suffers. Jesus is God. What Jesus suffered, God suffered.

A powerful moment in the movie *The Passion of the Christ* occurs when Jesus, overwhelmed with pain and exhaustion, lies on the ground as guards kick, mock, and spit on him. A horrified woman, her hand outstretched, pleads, "Someone, stop this!"

The great irony is that "Someone," God's Son, was doing something unspeakably great that required it *not* be stopped. Had someone delivered Jesus from his suffering that day, he could not have delivered us from ours.

God ordained and allowed all this—Jesus' temporary suffering—so he could prevent our eternal suffering.

Lord, thank you for fulfilling Job's ancient longing for someone to bridge the gap between you and us in your incarnation and atonement as the God-man, whose suffering far eclipsed Job's and ours. Thank you for knowing, for caring, and for fully understanding our suffering and that your suffering bought what will mean the final end of ours.

23

The Gospel Truth

But he was pierced for our transgressions,
 he was crushed for our iniquities;
the punishment that brought us peace was upon him,
 and by his wounds we are healed.
We all, like sheep, have gone astray,
 each of us has turned to his own way;
and the LORD has laid on him
 the iniquity of us all.
He was oppressed and afflicted,
 yet he did not open his mouth;
he was led like a lamb to the slaughter,
 and as a sheep before her shearers is silent,
 so he did not open his mouth.
By oppression and judgment he was taken away.
 And who can speak of his descendants?
For he was cut off from the land of the living;
 for the transgression of my people he was stricken.

    —ISAIAH 53:5–8

As an unbeliever raised with no knowledge of God, I was drawn to Christ in part because New Testament accounts of the Atonement, anticipated seven hundred years earlier in Isaiah 53, seemed so contrary to typical human reasoning. Yet I found them completely credible. No human would make up such a story! It had (and still has) the ring of truth.

Sometimes our familiarity with the gospel story prevents us from understanding its breathtaking nature. That's one benefit of reading other redemptive stories that give us glimpses of the greatest one. To me, C. S. Lewis's *The Lion, the Witch and the Wardrobe* offers particular help in understanding Christ's atoning sacrifice.

Aslan, the all-powerful lion, created Narnia and all worlds. After Lucy hears that her brother has to die for his treachery, she asks Aslan, "Can anything be done to save Edmund?"

"All shall be done," Aslan responds. "But it may be harder than you think." Knowing the terrible suffering and death that await him, Aslan becomes very sad. But he can save Edmund only through his self-sacrifice.

Those serving Aslan's foe, the White Witch, roll Aslan onto his back and tie his paws together. "Had the Lion chosen, one of those paws could have been the death of them all," C. S. Lewis writes. Finally, the witch orders that Aslan, their rightful king, be shaved. They cut off his beautiful mane and ridicule him. Aslan surrenders to his enemies, trading his life for Edmund's.[17]

Likewise, Jesus felt overwhelming sadness in the Garden of Gethsemane. He told his disciples, "My soul is crushed with grief to the point of death. Stay here and keep watch with me" (Matthew 26:38, NLT). The soldiers who guarded Jesus mocked him and hit him (see

Luke 22:63). And in actual history, Jesus went to the cross to die for us. That's how much he loves us.

The drama of evil and suffering in Christ's sacrifice addresses the very heart of the problem of evil and suffering. One day it will prove to have been the final answer.

Thank you, Father, that Christ's redemptive work guarantees the ultimate end of evil and suffering among your people. Thank you for Isaiah's prophecy, which anticipated Messiah's redemptive work. Thank you for C. S. Lewis's portrayal of Aslan, who allows us a powerful sidelong glimpse at the power, grace, and sacrificial love of our Jesus.

24

God Understands

For it is commendable if a man bears up under the pain of unjust suffering because he is conscious of God. But how is it to your credit if you receive a beating for doing wrong and endure it? But if you suffer for doing good and you endure it, this is commendable before God. To this you were called, because Christ suffered for you, leaving you an example, that you should follow in his steps.

"He committed no sin,

and no deceit was found in his mouth."

When they hurled their insults at him, he did not retaliate; when he suffered, he made no threats. Instead, he entrusted himself to him who judges justly. He himself bore our sins in his body on the tree, so that we might die to sins and live for righteousness; by his wounds you have been healed. For you were like sheep going astray, but now you have returned to the Shepherd and Overseer of your souls.

—1 PETER 2:19–25

S uffering is bad. Unjust suffering seems, at times, intolerable. It is not just painful; it is *wrong*.

Twenty years ago, I was named in an unwarranted lawsuit. In court, some of the plaintiffs—the owner and staff of an abortion clinic—falsely accused me and others of yelling and swearing at women, calling them names, and putting our hands on them as they attempted to enter the abortion clinic. When a Portland pastor testified that he had watched as we quietly and peacefully stood in front of the door, blocking access to the place where innocent children were being killed, the judge's anger erupted. Finally the judge issued a directed verdict. He told the jury they *must* find us guilty and choose a punitive amount sufficient to deter us from ever coming to the clinic again. The judgment against us was $8.2 million, the largest in history against a group of peaceful protesters.

My single greatest encouragement during that time was 1 Peter 2, which says of Jesus, "When he suffered, he made no threats. Instead, he entrusted himself to him who judges justly" (verse 23). Repeatedly I reminded myself that there is only one Judge, only one Supreme Court of the universe. Ultimately it was not the unrighteous judge sitting before us but God himself whom I would answer to. And in the end, not in this life but in the life to come, that one Righteous Judge would make all things right.

In fact, the injustice against Jesus spoken of in 1 Peter 2 culminated in his crucifixion, a hideous injustice that makes all others pale in comparison. And it was the undeserved suffering of Christ on the cross that brought about my redemption. Had he not suffered unjustly on my behalf, and done so with his eyes on his Father, I would be spending eternity in Hell, along with you and everyone else.

Everything before the Cross points forward to it. Everything since the Cross points back to it. Everything that will last was purchased on it. Everything that matters hinges on it.

In all human history, who has paid the highest price for evil and suffering? Poll a hundred people on this question, and only a few would come up with the right answer: *God*.

"This is love: not that we loved God, but that he loved us and sent his Son as an atoning sacrifice for our sins" (1 John 4:10). If you and I had witnessed firsthand Gethsemane and the march to Golgotha and the horrors of the Cross, we'd never question for a moment either God's empathy or love. (He has recorded those events in his Word that we might see them in our mind's eye; if we do, our preoccupation with the injustices done against us will inevitably diminish.)

God paid the highest price on our behalf; we have no grounds for believing he doesn't "get it." He knows what it's like to watch his Son die. One thing we must never say about God is that he doesn't understand what it means to be utterly abandoned, suffer terribly, and die miserably.

Jesus suffered the same trials and temptations we do. God understands our worst losses and heartbreaks, even our temptations: "Because he himself suffered when he was tempted, he is able to help those who are being tempted" (Hebrews 2:18).

Dorothy Sayers wrote:

For whatever reason God chose to make man as he is—
limited and suffering and subject to sorrows and death—
God had the honesty and the courage to take his own
medicine. Whatever game he is playing with his creation,

he has kept his own rules and played fair. He can exact nothing from man that he has not exacted from himself. He has himself gone through the whole of human experience, from the trivial irritations of family life and the cramping restrictions of hard work and lack of money to the worst horrors of pain and humiliation, defeat, despair, and death. When he was a man, he played the man. He was born in poverty and died in disgrace and thought it well worthwhile.[18]

God calls us to hold firmly to our faith precisely because he knows suffering and temptation from firsthand experience.

Thank you, my Jesus, that you are no stranger to suffering and that the worst day of my life has been far better than your worst day. Thank you for entrusting yourself to your Father, the righteous Judge of the universe, in your darkest hour. As you pray for me now in Heaven, please pray that I will follow your example, empowered by your Holy Spirit.

25

The Sentence Against God

He was assigned a grave with the wicked,
    and with the rich in his death,
though he had done no violence,
    nor was any deceit in his mouth.
Yet it was the LORD's will to crush him and cause him to
        suffer,
    and though the LORD makes his life a guilt offering,
he will see his offspring and prolong his days,
    and the will of the LORD will prosper in his hand.
After the suffering of his soul,
    he will see the light of life and be satisfied;
by his knowledge my righteous servant will justify many,
    and he will bear their iniquities.
Therefore I will give him a portion among the great,
    and he will divide the spoils with the strong,
because he poured out his life unto death,
    and was numbered with the transgressors.
For he bore the sin of many,
    and made intercession for the transgressors.

—ISAIAH 53:9–12

I saiah's prophecies were fulfilled with shocking accuracy seven centuries later, as Christ went to the cross to bear our sins, was crucified between two thieves, and prayed for those calling for his blood.

John Stott, in *The Cross of Christ,* tells a story about billions of people seated on a great plain before God's throne. Most shrank back, while some crowded to the front, raising angry voices.

"Can God judge us? How can he know about suffering?" snapped one woman, ripping a sleeve to reveal a tattooed number from a Nazi concentration camp. "We endured terror…beatings…torture…death!"

Other sufferers expressed their complaints against God for the evil and suffering he had permitted. What did God know of weeping, hunger, and hatred? God leads a sheltered life in Heaven, they said.

Someone from Hiroshima, people born deformed, others murdered, each sent forward a representative. They concluded that before God could judge them, he should be sentenced to live on Earth as a man to endure the suffering they had endured. Then they pronounced a sentence:

> Let him be born a Jew. Let the legitimacy of his birth be doubted. Let his close friends betray him. Let him face false charges. Let a prejudiced jury try him and a cowardly judge convict him. Let him be tortured. Let him be utterly alone. Then, bloody and forsaken, let him die.
>
> The room grew silent after the sentence against God had been pronounced. No one moved, and a weight fell on each face.
>
> For suddenly, all knew that God already had served his sentence.[19]

That God did this willingly, with ancient premeditation, is all the more astonishing. Some people can't believe God would create a world in which people would suffer so much. Isn't it more remarkable that God would create a world in which no one would suffer more than he did?

Lord, the Cross was no afterthought! Thank you for planning it from before the world's beginning and foretelling it centuries in advance. Thank you for never dishing out suffering without taking far more upon yourself. While we have no choice but to suffer in this life, you did have a choice and elected to suffer for our sins so we don't have to in eternity. Words cannot capture the shocking nature of your redemptive work. Saying thank you is not nearly enough. But it is at least a place to begin.

26

Forsaken for a Reason

At the sixth hour darkness came over the whole land until the ninth hour. And at the ninth hour Jesus cried out in a loud voice, *"Eloi, Eloi, lama sabachthani?"*—which means, "My God, my God, why have you forsaken me?"

When some of those standing near heard this, they said, "Listen, he's calling Elijah."

One man ran, filled a sponge with wine vinegar, put it on a stick, and offered it to Jesus to drink. "Now leave him alone. Let's see if Elijah comes to take him down," he said.

With a loud cry, Jesus breathed his last.

The curtain of the temple was torn in two from top to bottom. And when the centurion, who stood there in front of Jesus, heard his cry and saw how he died, he said, "Surely this man was the Son of God!"

—MARK 15:33–39

Echoing David in Psalm 22, Jesus cried out on the cross, "My God, my God, why have you forsaken me?" In that haunting cry, Christ identifies with our despair and bridges the gap between God and us not only theologically, in the Atonement, but emotionally—between our suffering and God's, between our agonizing cries and those of God's Son.

The beloved Son who had "well pleased" his Father (Matthew 3:17) *became* our sin (see 2 Corinthians 5:21). So the Father turned away. For the first time in all eternity, the oneness within the Godhead knew separation. In ways we cannot comprehend—ways that would amount to blasphemy had not God revealed it to us—the Atonement somehow tore God apart.

Some believe that Jesus' cry showed he didn't know why his Father had poured out his wrath on him. But Scripture says otherwise. Anticipating his death, Jesus said, "Now my heart is troubled, and what shall I say? 'Father, save me from this hour'? No, it was for this very reason I came to this hour. Father, glorify your name!" (John 12:27–28). Jesus knew why he had to die. He cried out because any separation from his Father constituted an infinite horror.

Tim Keller explains:

The physical pain was nothing compared to the spiritual experience of cosmic abandonment. Christianity alone among the world religions claims that God became uniquely and fully human in Jesus Christ and therefore knows firsthand despair, rejection, loneliness, poverty, bereavement, torture, and imprisonment. On the Cross he went beyond even the worst human suffering and experienced cosmic rejection and pain that exceeds ours as infinitely as his knowledge and power exceeds ours.[20]

The unrighteous have no grounds for asking God why he has forsaken them—all who understand his holiness and our sin know the reasons. But God's beloved Son had the right to ask, even knowing the answer. In some qualitative—not quantitative—way, Jesus endured the punishment of Hell. When he said, "It is finished," signaling he had paid the redemptive price, Jesus ceased to bear the penalty for our sin. Then "Jesus called out with a loud voice, 'Father, into your hands I commit my spirit.' When he had said this, he breathed his last" (Luke 23:46). The unimaginable had happened. But once redemption was accomplished in space-time history, the triune God was restored to the complete oneness known from eternity past and assured for eternity future.

Lord, nothing is so horrifying as the teaching of Scripture that you became sin for us and in doing so became the object of your Father's wrath. Thank you, Father, for being there for Jesus as he went to the cross and as his spirit departed from his body on the cross. But thank you too—Father and Son and Holy Spirit together—for your willingness, in those three hours of unfathomable darkness, to make the ultimate sacrifice to purchase our place with you forever.

27

Jesus Changes Everything

Two other men, both criminals, were also led out with him to be executed. When they came to the place called the Skull, there they crucified him, along with the criminals—one on his right, the other on his left. Jesus said, "Father, forgive them, for they do not know what they are doing." And they divided up his clothes by casting lots.

The people stood watching, and the rulers even sneered at him. They said, "He saved others; let him save himself if he is the Christ of God, the Chosen One."

The soldiers also came up and mocked him. They offered him wine vinegar and said, "If you are the king of the Jews, save yourself."

There was a written notice above him, which read: THIS IS THE KING OF THE JEWS.

One of the criminals who hung there hurled insults at him: "Aren't you the Christ? Save yourself and us!"

But the other criminal rebuked him. "Don't you fear God," he said, "since you are under the same sentence? We are punished justly, for we are getting what our deeds deserve. But this man has done nothing wrong."

Then he said, "Jesus, remember me when you come into your kingdom."

Jesus answered him, "I tell you the truth, today you will be with me in paradise."

—LUKE 23:32–43

They sneered at Jesus, mocked him, and insulted him. Yet one of the thieves who saw him for who he was, said that—unlike himself—Jesus was innocent, and sought his blessing. Despite his agony, Jesus took the time to promise the thief that Paradise awaited him on the other side of his suffering.

If I had to believe that what we now see represents God's best for this world, I would not be a Christian. If not for the redemptive work of Christ, I would not believe in God's goodness. The fault would lie with me, for God would remain good even if he hadn't gone to the cross for us. But no matter how persuasive the argument that we sinners deserve judgment, I couldn't overcome the obstacles of suffering children or slaughters like the Holocaust and the Killing Fields.

That Jesus Christ, the eternal Son of God, would choose to endure the cross to pay for sin, that he would take on the sufferings of *all* people at Golgotha, changed the way I look at suffering and evil and how they reflect upon God's character.

The proven character of Christ, demonstrated in his sacrifice on our behalf, makes him trustworthy even when evil and suffering overwhelm us.

For me, Jesus changes everything.

The Bible describes Christ in the garden before he went to the cross: "Being in anguish, he prayed more earnestly, and his sweat was like drops of blood falling to the ground" (Luke 22:44). The enormous stress upon him broke his blood vessels. He chose to die for our evils, to be alienated from his Father, to bear an emotional pain that exceeded even his physical misery.

Bloody, realistic imagery disturbed many who watched the movie *The Passion of the Christ*. But Christ's very worst suffering on the cross—his bearing of sins that separated him from the loving presence of his Father—no one could capture on screen.

How could he endure such suffering for us? And why, since he has done so, would I ever accuse or reject him?

Whenever you feel tempted to ask God, "Why did you do this *to* me?" look at the cross and ask, "Why did you do that *for* me?"

Lord, as we face our suffering, remind us of yours. You were the King before you went to the cross and as you hung upon it. You offered pardon and Paradise to a sinner, and three days later you conquered death for him and for us. Words cannot express the extent of our debt to you or our gratitude. You changed everything for that thief on the cross. Thank you for changing everything for me.

28

Christ's Own Choice

Therefore Jesus said again, "I tell you the truth, I am the gate for the sheep. All who ever came before me were thieves and robbers, but the sheep did not listen to them. I am the gate; whoever enters through me will be saved. He will come in and go out, and find pasture. The thief comes only to steal and kill and destroy; I have come that they may have life, and have it to the full.

"I am the good shepherd. The good shepherd lays down his life for the sheep. The hired hand is not the shepherd who owns the sheep. So when he sees the wolf coming, he abandons the sheep and runs away. Then the wolf attacks the flock and scatters it. The man runs away because he is a hired hand and cares nothing for the sheep.

"I am the good shepherd; I know my sheep and my sheep know me—just as the Father knows me and I know the Father—and I lay down my life for the sheep. I have other sheep that are not of this sheep pen. I must bring them also. They too will listen to my voice, and there shall be one flock and one shepherd. The reason my Father loves me is that I lay down my life—only to take it up again. No one takes it from me, but I lay it down of my own accord. I have authority to lay it down and authority to take it up again. This command I received from my Father."

—JOHN 10:7–18

Jesus was no one's victim: "I lay down my life.… No one takes it from me, but I lay it down of my own accord." It's one thing to suffer terribly, another to *choose* to suffer terribly. In his love for us, God self-imposed the death sentence. Later, upon being arrested, he said, "Do you think I cannot call on my Father, and he will at once put at my disposal more than twelve legions of angels? But how then would the Scriptures be fulfilled that say it must happen in this way?" (Matthew 26:53–54). He submitted willingly to humiliating torture and execution, fulfilling his Father's will to win our salvation. God's Son bore no guilt of his own; he bore ours alone.

The temptation to end it all must have been overwhelming. With no more than a thought, just the unspoken word *Come,* Christ could have called upon waiting armies to strike down his torturers and bring him instant relief. Perhaps the greatest wonder is not that Jesus *went* to the cross but that he *stayed* on it.

Why did Jesus hang on it for six hours rather than six seconds or six minutes? Perhaps as a reminder that suffering is a process. God does not end our suffering as soon as we would like. He did not end his Son's suffering as soon as he would have liked. We stand in good company.

Christ foresaw the good even as he faced the bad, and that helped him to endure. He is the one "who for the joy set before him endured the cross, scorning its shame, and sat down at the right hand of the throne of God" (Hebrews 12:2).

If God brought eternal joy through the suffering of Jesus, can he bring eternal joy through my present suffering and yours? If Jesus endured his suffering through anticipating the reward of unending joy, can he empower you and me to do the same?

Lord, thank you for being the Good Shepherd who laid down your life for your sheep. We praise you that you were no one's victim, that you deliberately and intentionally gave your life as the Lamb who takes away the sins of the world.

29

Shared Suffering

All of you, clothe yourselves with humility toward one another, because,

"God opposes the proud
    but gives grace to the humble."
Humble yourselves, therefore, under God's mighty hand, that he may lift you up in due time. Cast all your anxiety on him because he cares for you.

Be self-controlled and alert. Your enemy the devil prowls around like a roaring lion looking for someone to devour. Resist him, standing firm in the faith, because you know that your brothers throughout the world are undergoing the same kind of sufferings.

And the God of all grace, who called you to his eternal glory in Christ, after you have suffered a little while, will himself restore you and make you strong, firm and steadfast. To him be the power for ever and ever. Amen.

—1 PETER 5:5–11

We are not alone in our suffering. Jesus suffered for us, he suffers with us, and our brothers and sisters throughout the world suffer alongside us as we follow our suffering Savior.

When we lock our eyes on our cancer, arthritis, fibromyalgia, diabetes, or disability, self-pity and bitterness can creep in. When we spend our days rehearsing the tragic death of a loved one, we will interpret all of life through the darkness of our suffering. How much better to focus upon Jesus!

"Let us fix our eyes on Jesus...who for the joy set before him endured the cross." The following verse commands us: "Consider him who endured such opposition from sinful men, so that you will not grow weary and lose heart" (Hebrews 12:2–3).

However great our suffering, his was far greater. If you feel angry at God, what price would you have him pay for his failure to do more for people facing suffering and evil? Would you inflict capital punishment on him? You're too late. No matter how bitter we feel toward God, could any of us come up with a punishment worse than what God chose to inflict upon himself?

Tim Keller writes:

If we again ask the question: "Why does God allow evil and suffering to continue?" and we look at the cross of Jesus, we still do not know what the answer is. However, we know what the answer isn't. It can't be that he doesn't love us. It can't be that he is indifferent or detached from our condition. God takes our misery and suffering *so* seriously that he was willing to take it on himself.... So, if we embrace the Christian teaching that Jesus is God and that he went to the Cross, then we have deep consolation and strength to face the brutal realities of life on earth.[21]

If you know Jesus, then the hand holding yours bears the calluses of a carpenter who carried a cross for you. When he opens his hand, you see the gnarled flesh of the nail scars on his wrists. And when you think he doesn't understand your pain, realize that you don't understand the extent of his. Love him or not, he has proven he loves you.

In your most troubled moments, when you cry out to God, "Why have you let this happen?" picture the outstretched hands of Christ, forever scarred…for you.

Do those look like the hands of a God who does not care?

When doubts assail us, Lord, when the reality of your love starts to fade from view, remind us of your human hands, with the calluses of a carpenter and the scars of a Savior. Lord, what more can we ask from you than what you have done for us and what you promise you will yet do?

30

Creator of *All*

I am the LORD, and there is no other;
 apart from me there is no God.
I will strengthen you,
 though you have not acknowledged me,
so that from the rising of the sun
 to the place of its setting
men may know there is none besides me.
 I am the LORD, and there is no other.
I form the light and create darkness,
 I bring prosperity and create disaster;
 I, the LORD, do all these things.
You heavens above, rain down righteousness;
 let the clouds shower it down.
Let the earth open wide,
 let salvation spring up,
let righteousness grow with it;
 I, the LORD, have created it.

—ISAIAH 45:5–8

How can a good God be said in the Bible to not only form the light but also to create darkness? How can he not only bring prosperity but also create disaster? How can we even begin to wrap our minds around such things? Perhaps we can begin by reminding ourselves that God calls upon us to believe what he has said, even when we don't understand it.

Scripture sometimes regards physical afflictions as consequences of the Fall, sometimes as the work of demons, but sometimes just as clearly attributes them to God.

God said to Moses, "Who gave man his mouth? Who makes him deaf or mute? Who gives him sight or makes him blind? Is it not I, the LORD?" (Exodus 4:11). Remarkably, God takes full credit here for giving disabilities. God doesn't say the Fall makes people deaf, the Curse makes them mute, or Satan makes them blind. God says that *he* does. He doesn't attempt to give a full list. But doesn't he clearly intend us to understand that he also gives people Down syndrome, deformities, cancer, and diabetes? Just because we don't like the idea that deformities, diseases, and suffering come from God's own hand does not alter Scripture. Our discomfort will not change God's mind. We don't get a vote.

Many Christians deliberately distance God from disabilities and diseases, sometimes arguing that people won't trust a God who would deliberately dispense such things. Yet I have spoken with disabled people who didn't find comfort until they finally came to believe that God had made them as they are.

Right-thinking believers find reassurance in knowing that such life-altering abnormalities don't happen randomly or because of bad luck but are granted to us with divine purpose. God doesn't helplessly watch us suffer because of bad genes, an accident caused by Satan, or careless or evil people. Rather, he offers us help in dealing with any disability he has given us.

I've seen clearly how God has used my insulin-dependent diabetes to humble me. It's no accident that it appeared the same month my first book came out in 1985. God wanted me to depend on him. A half dozen or more times every day, I am reminded of my need.

If we see God's involvement in people's deformity or disease, we will view them differently than if we think they suffer because of Satan or sin. Whether we believe that *God* makes the Down syndrome, Trisomy 18, or anencephalic children as they are profoundly affects our hearts toward them. A large percentage of children diagnosed with diseases before birth are aborted. If we believe that Satan alone deforms the child or gives the adult a disease, then we might view taking their lives as battling evil instead of committing it. If we believe that God has made these individuals as they are, then we can love them as he intends.

God, despite the horrific reality of humankind's fall, the Curse, and the devil's rebellion, you do not abdicate your throne but call yourself the Creator of even our disabilities. This seems hard to take at first, but it's comforting in the end, for it means that the adversity we face is not outside your plan and purposes but part of them. Help us to look

at others with their disabilities and diseases, and the weakness and vulnerability of being preborn or aged, and see them not as expendable embarrassments but as precious people made in your image and deserving of our greatest respect and care.

31

Second-Guessing God

Woe to him who quarrels with his Maker,
    to him who is but a potsherd among the potsherds on the
    ground.
Does the clay say to the potter,
    "What are you making?"
Does your work say,
    "He has no hands"?
Woe to him who says to his father,
    "What have you begotten?"
or to his mother,
    "What have you brought to birth?"
This is what the LORD says—
    the Holy One of Israel, and its Maker:
Concerning things to come,
    do you question me about my children,
    or give me orders about the work of my hands?
It is I who made the earth
    and created mankind upon it.
My own hands stretched out the heavens;
    I marshaled their starry hosts.

              —ISAIAH 45:9–12

It's hard to imagine a more humorously bizarre spectacle than a piece of pottery arguing with its maker about its size, shape, and functions. While as humans we're far more valuable than pottery, the point is that we are no more qualified to second-guess our Creator than a piece of clay is to judge its potter.

Vicki Anderson was born with hypertelorism, a facial abnormality. Vicki says:

> I don't really like the phrase "birth defect"—it contradicts my theology. A "defect" infers a mistake and I believe that God is sovereign. If he had the power to create the entire universe according to his exact specifications, then my face was certainly no challenge for him!... If God is loving, why did he deform my face? I don't know—maybe because with a normal face I would have been robbed of the thousands and thousands of blessings that I have received because of my deformities. It seems odd, but usually our greatest trial is what most molds and shapes us. It gives us character, backbone, courage, wisdom, discernment, and friendships that are not shallow.[22]

My friend David O'Brien, who has had a severe form of cerebral palsy since birth, once spoke with me at a conference for disabled people. David pointed out that God didn't merely say he *permitted* deafness and blindness but that he *created* people with those conditions (see Exodus 4:11). Then David said, "God knows the spirit and will in each person, and he shapes the body to mold that will to his purpose. A gardener uses gradual tension to shape a tree into a beautiful arch. A special body is the gradual tension that shapes spirit and will to glorify God."

Then, as David and I stood in front of our disabled brothers and sisters, he said something unforgettable: "Dare I question God's wisdom in making me the way I am? If God knew that Christ had to suffer to make him complete, certainly he knows what I need."

David ended his presentation with these words: "I'm sure that if I were not handicapped, I would not be here with you. Actually, I would probably be out on a racetrack driving the fastest car I could find."

Laughter erupted. But David had made his point: his disability kept him from doing many things. And while there's nothing wrong with racing a car (and I wouldn't be surprised to see David drive one on the New Earth), such a distraction might have become his life's focus and kept him from Christ. Deprived of lesser objects of affection, he turned to the greatest: Jesus Christ.

Skeptics may say of these disabled people, "They're denying reality and finding false comfort. If there's a God who loves them, he wouldn't treat them like this."

But those at the conference found better reasons to believe and worship the God who purchased their resurrection with his blood and offers them comfort and perspective, than reasons to believe the skeptics who've purchased them nothing and offer them only hopelessness.

Thank you, Lord, our Creator, for knowing what's best.
You accomplish a million things invisible to us for every one

thing we see and understand. You are always on the job, behind the scenes, where it takes faith for us to believe it. Your purposes are set, you designed us wisely, and our disabilities and diseases and "accidents" never take you by surprise and never thwart your plans. Give us comfort in the knowledge that you have a purpose even in the hardest circumstances.

32

God's Good Work

We ourselves, who have the firstfruits of the Spirit, groan inwardly as we wait eagerly for our adoption as sons, the redemption of our bodies. For in this hope we were saved. But hope that is seen is no hope at all. Who hopes for what he already has? But if we hope for what we do not yet have, we wait for it patiently.

In the same way, the Spirit helps us in our weakness. We do not know what we ought to pray for, but the Spirit himself intercedes for us with groans that words cannot express. And he who searches our hearts knows the mind of the Spirit, because the Spirit intercedes for the saints in accordance with God's will.

And we know that in all things God works for the good of those who love him, who have been called according to his purpose. For those God foreknew he also predestined to be conformed to the likeness of his Son, that he might be the firstborn among many brothers. And those he predestined, he also called; those he called, he also justified; those he justified, he also glorified.

—ROMANS 8:23–30

P aul, having spoken about a world groaning in its suffering, says, "We *know* that in all things God works for the good of those who love him" (Romans 8:28). How can we know something so incredible? Because we know God is both sovereign and loving. We know he is fully in charge and he is lovingly carrying out a plan not only for his ultimate glory but for our ultimate good.

Benjamin B. Warfield, world-renowned theologian, taught at Princeton Seminary for thirty-four years until his death in 1921. Students still read his books today. But most of them don't know that in 1876, at age twenty-five, he married Annie Kinkead. They traveled to Germany for their honeymoon. In an intense thunderstorm, lightning struck Annie and permanently paralyzed her (some biographers are uncertain of this but believe nonetheless she was traumatized by the storm, with permanent physical results). After Warfield cared for her for thirty-nine years, she died in 1915. Because of her extreme needs, Warfield seldom left his home for more than two hours at a time during all those years of marriage.[23]

Imagine your marriage beginning like that on your honeymoon. Imagine how it might affect your worldview. So what did this theologian with shattered dreams have to say about Romans 8:28?

> The fundamental thought is the universal government of
> God. All that comes to you is under His controlling hand.
> The secondary thought is the favour of God to those that love
> Him. If He governs all, then nothing but good can befall
> those to whom He would do good.… Though we are too
> weak to help ourselves and too blind to ask for what we need,
> and can only groan in unformed longings, He is the author in

us of these very longings…and He will so govern all things
that we shall reap only good from all that befalls us.[24]

Really, Dr. Warfield? *Only* good from *all* that befalls us? Even
from a personal tragedy that deeply hurts your beloved wife and dramatically restricts her personal liberties and your daily schedule for the
rest of her life and for most of yours? Warfield spoke not from the
sidelines but from the playing field of suffering, answering an emphatic "Yes!" to the loving sovereignty of God.

Paul wrote Romans 8:28 from a long track record of hardship,
beatings, shipwrecks, cold, hunger, and sorrow. He had just spoken of
the sufferings of this present time and the groanings of all creation,
from God's children and the Holy Spirit himself. Paul brought solid
credentials of adversity to the writing of Romans 8:28. Countless
people such as B. B. Warfield have affirmed the same truth, earning
the right to do so in the school of suffering.

If we see God as he really is, as he is revealed in Scripture, we can
trust in his loving sovereignty even in life's greatest hardships.

God, we are grateful that our faith is not based on wish-
ful thinking or today's circumstances. As you did for Dr.
Warfield, help us ground our faith in the bedrock of your
unchanging character and the reality of your love for us,
testified to in Scripture and indisputably proven in the
Cross of Jesus.

33

Making the Best of the Worst

Consider it pure joy, my brothers, whenever you face trials of many kinds, because you know that the testing of your faith develops perseverance. Perseverance must finish its work so that you may be mature and complete, not lacking anything. If any of you lacks wisdom, he should ask God, who gives generously to all without finding fault, and it will be given to him. But when he asks, he must believe and not doubt, because he who doubts is like a wave of the sea, blown and tossed by the wind. That man should not think he will receive anything from the Lord; he is a double-minded man, unstable in all he does.

The brother in humble circumstances ought to take pride in his high position. But the one who is rich should take pride in his low position, because he will pass away like a wild flower. For the sun rises with scorching heat and withers the plant; its blossom falls and its beauty is destroyed. In the same way, the rich man will fade away even while he goes about his business.

Blessed is the man who perseveres under trial, because when he has stood the test, he will receive the crown of life that God has promised to those who love him.

—JAMES 1:2–12

F ind joy in the midst of trials? Persevere under adversity? Do these seem like things only super-Christians could do and an impossible dream for the rest of us?

Take a closer look at your own life, and you may catch a glimpse of exactly what Scripture is talking about. Because if you consider the best and the worst things that have happened to you, you may see a startling overlap.

Fold a paper in half. Then write on the top half the worst things that have happened to you and on the bottom half the best.

Invariably, if you've lived long enough, if enough time has passed since some of those "worst things" happened to you, then you'll almost certainly find an overlap. Experiences labeled as the worst things that ever happened, *over time* become some of the best. That's because God uses the painful, difficult experiences of life for our ultimate good.

How is this possible? Because God is both loving and sovereign. Our lists provide persuasive proof that while evil and suffering are not good, God can use them to accomplish immeasurable good. This knowledge should give us great confidence that even when we don't see any redemptive meaning in our suffering, *God* can see it—and one day we will too. Therefore, we need not run from suffering or lose hope if God doesn't remove it. We can trust that God has a purpose for whatever he permits.

Perhaps the greatest test of whether we believe Romans 8:28— "In all things God works for the good of those who love him, who have been called according to his purpose"—is to identify the very worst things that have happened to us, then ask if we believe that in the end God will somehow use them for our good.

Reflecting on his long life, Malcolm Muggeridge wrote:

Contrary to what might be expected, I look back on experiences that at the time seemed especially desolating and painful with particular satisfaction. Indeed, I can say with complete truthfulness that everything I have learned in my seventy-five years in this world, everything that has truly enhanced and enlightened my existence, has been through affliction and not through happiness, whether pursued or attained.[25]

Lord, we look back at things that, at the time, seemed to bring only bad—not an ounce of good. Yet in time, we see how you used job loss, an accident, a disease, a false accusation, the death of a friend, a public humiliation, an addiction, or even the end of a marriage to build character and increase dependence on you and to get a fresh start in our walk with you. Help us ponder how you've already brought good out of some of the bad to fuel our faith that one day you will bring yet greater good out of all of the bad.

34

Meaningful Choice, Real Consequences

See, I set before you today life and prosperity, death and destruction. For I command you today to love the LORD your God, to walk in his ways, and to keep his commands, decrees and laws; then you will live and increase, and the LORD your God will bless you in the land you are entering to possess.

But if your heart turns away and you are not obedient, and if you are drawn away to bow down to other gods and worship them, I declare to you this day that you will certainly be destroyed. You will not live long in the land you are crossing the Jordan to enter and possess.

This day I call heaven and earth as witnesses against you that I have set before you life and death, blessings and curses. Now choose life, so that you and your children may live and that you may love the LORD your God, listen to his voice, and hold fast to him. For the LORD is your life, and he will give you many years in the land he swore to give to your fathers, Abraham, Isaac and Jacob.

—DEUTERONOMY 30:15–20

In his revealed Word, God sets before us clear paths—the way of life and the way of death, the way of blessings and the way of curses, the wise way and the foolish way. Then he says to us today, as much as to his children Israel long ago, "Choose life.... For the LORD is your life."

What sane person would choose death over life, bringing terrible harm to himself and his family and neighbors? Yet sinners make such choices, for there is an insanity to sin.

I've heard people argue that a good and all-powerful God should miraculously prevent every harmful event.

But a world of freedom requires cause and effect. Miracles must be the exception, not the rule. Otherwise, our choices would have no real consequences. I could step off the top of a tall building or hit someone with a baseball bat without fear of the cost, since God would prevent the consequences from my bad choices. (And therefore I would not see them as bad.)

The nature of wood, which allows us to use it as a baseball bat, also allows us to use it as a murder weapon. C. S. Lewis invited us to imagine a world structured so that wooden beams would become soft as grass when used as a weapon and sound waves would not carry lies or insults:

> But such a world would be one in which wrong actions were impossible, and in which, therefore, freedom of the will would be void.... Try to exclude the possibility of suffering which the order of nature and the existence of free-wills involve, and you find that you have excluded life itself.[26]

If God disarmed every shooter and prevented every drunk driver from crashing, this would not be a real world in which people make consequential choices. It would not be a world of character development and faith building. It would not be a world where families put their arms around one another to face life's difficulties. It would be a world where people went blithely along with their lives, content to do evil and put up with it, feeling no need to turn to God, no incentive to consider the gospel and prepare for eternity. In such a world, people would die without a sense of need, only to find themselves in Hell.

The present but temporary evil and suffering of this world are compatible with a God who despises evil but values the freedom necessary for meaningful choice. God desires significant and therefore consequential relationships with his creatures, and that requires some freedom on our part. If God were to eliminate choice or its consequences, it would mean eliminating people, marriage, family, and culture and would bring to an end the meaningful life of all God's creatures. Apparently, in his wisdom, God decided it wasn't worth the price.

Father, we look at this world and see much that is good, some that is wonderful, but also much that frightens us and breaks our hearts. We love having the freedom to choose, but as sinners and rebels we have abused it terribly. Help us trust you when you say that our suffering will be worthwhile because of the redemptive magnificence we will celebrate for eternity.

35

God, the Wise Judge

O righteous God,
    who searches minds and hearts,
bring to an end the violence of the wicked
    and make the righteous secure.
My shield is God Most High,
    who saves the upright in heart.
God is a righteous judge,
    a God who expresses his wrath every day.
If he does not relent,
    he will sharpen his sword;
    he will bend and string his bow.
He has prepared his deadly weapons;
    he makes ready his flaming arrows.
He who is pregnant with evil
    and conceives trouble gives birth to disillusionment.
He who digs a hole and scoops it out
    falls into the pit he has made.
The trouble he causes recoils on himself;
    his violence comes down on his own head.

I will give thanks to the LORD because of his righteousness
and will sing praise to the name of the LORD Most High.
—PSALM 7:9–17

G od is unfailingly righteous, exercising his wrath selectively each
day and poising himself to bring final judgment upon unrepentant evildoers. Therefore God's children should rejoice, knowing that
his enemies and theirs will ultimately not get away with anything.

When a dear friend of ours was raped, God remained sovereign—
but I believe his fierce anger erupted at the evil done to this precious
woman, his beloved daughter. He is the God who says, "I myself will
fight...with an outstretched hand and a mighty arm in anger and fury
and great wrath" (Jeremiah 21:5).

God hated the crime done against our friend, but it's also true
that he could have stopped the rape and in so doing prevented much
heartache. Yet, if Romans 8:28 applies to the great groan-causing suffering that pervades the verses surrounding it, surely it applies to our
friend's suffering also. If God permits evils not randomly but with
deliberate purpose so that he will reverse the Curse and bring eternal
blessing, then even though we don't understand how, he deserves our
trust, not our attacks.

This friend told me, years after her trauma:

I discovered in myself a spirit of entitlement. I learned that
God was not going to go down my checklist of happiness and

fulfill it. I learned what it meant to surrender to his will. Before, I wanted certain gifts from him. Now I want him. I have thought, *If this was going to happen to someone, it was better for it to happen to me, with my faith in God, than to happen to a twelve-year-old or an elderly person or to anyone without Christ.* I have come through this with an absolute confidence in God. I know he will walk with me through the rest of my life. I have been through the valley of the shadow of death, and he was with me. Because he's been faithful in all I've gone through, I have less to be afraid of now.

We're puzzled sometimes because God could have shown his power by preventing tragedies and healing diseases but chose not to. We would prefer that God crush and remove evil this very moment, without allowing it to hurt us. But power isn't his sole attribute. He is also glorified in showing his wisdom. While his power gains immediate praise, his wisdom is seen over time. Sometimes in this life, and one day in his presence, we will marvel at his wisdom in using certain evils—in ways we could never have imagined—for our ultimate good.

Father, thank you for the promise that you are a righteous judge who will one day pass sentence with mercy upon the repentant and wrath upon the unrepentant. Thank you that even in this life we see foretastes of both. Give us patience to wait and faith to trust that you have a redemptive and eternity-enhancing purpose in whatever happens in our lives.

36

God's Purpose Prevails

Once you were alienated from God and were enemies in your minds because of your evil behavior. But now he has reconciled you by Christ's physical body through death to present you holy in his sight, without blemish and free from accusation—if you continue in your faith, established and firm, not moved from the hope held out in the gospel. This is the gospel that you heard and that has been proclaimed to every creature under heaven, and of which I, Paul, have become a servant.

Now I rejoice in what was suffered for you, and I fill up in my flesh what is still lacking in regard to Christ's afflictions, for the sake of his body, which is the church. I have become its servant by the commission God gave me to present to you the word of God in its fullness—the mystery that has been kept hidden for ages and generations, but is now disclosed to the saints. To them God has chosen to make known among the Gentiles the glorious riches of this mystery, which is Christ in you, the hope of glory.

We proclaim him, admonishing and teaching everyone with all wisdom, so that we may present everyone perfect in

Christ. To this end I labor, struggling with all his energy, which so powerfully works in me.

—COLOSSIANS 1:21–29

Paul said he rejoiced in his afflictions. Why? Because he understood the gospel, the good news that eclipses all else—Jesus Christ came into the world to redeem it, to extend his transforming grace and accomplish, without failure, his sovereign and loving purposes in the lives of his beloved children, for his eternal glory and our eternal good.

Joseph's brothers intended his suffering for evil; God intended it for good. Satan intended Job's suffering for evil; God intended it for good. Satan intended Jesus' suffering for evil; God intended it for good. Satan intended Paul's suffering for evil; God intended it for good. In each case, God's purpose prevailed.

Satan intends your suffering for evil; God intends it for good.

Whose purpose for your suffering will prevail? Whose purpose are you furthering?

Satan attempts to destroy your faith, while God invites you to draw near to him and draw upon his sovereign grace to sustain you.

If we truly recognize God's sovereignty even over Satan's work—not just by saying the words but by believing the truth—our perspective isn't merely altered, it's transformed.

Some Christians constantly assign this mishap to Satan, that one to evil people, another to themselves, still others to God. Sometimes they are right, but how can they be sure which is which? When in 2 Corinthians 12 Paul sees God at work to conform his character to Christ even through the thorn in the flesh he calls "a messenger of Satan" (verse 7), surely this means that God works through *everything* that comes our way, no matter whom it comes from. If God can use "a messenger of Satan" for good, then surely he can use a car accident, a stolen iPod, a fight with your friend, or your employer's unreasonable expectations for good.

Countless millions of choices and actions are contemplated every instant across this globe. Our all-knowing and all-powerful God chooses exactly which ones he will permit and not permit. Scripture suggests he does not permit evils arbitrarily but with specific purposes in mind. Everything he permits matches up with his wisdom and ultimately serves both his holiness and his love.

God "permitting" something, then, describes what is far stronger than it may sound. After all, whatever God permits actually happens; what he doesn't permit doesn't happen. And as Joni Eareckson Tada puts it, "God permits what he hates to achieve what he loves."[27]

You might not know whether demons or human genetics under the Fall or a doctor's poor decision or God's direct hand have brought about your disease, but you know as much as you need to—that God is sovereign, and whether he heals your body now or waits until the resurrection to heal you, he desires to achieve his own good purpose in you.

The question is, simply, will you trust him?

Lord, what an amazing revelation that you are at work in the worst of things, even something so bad as to be called a messenger from the devil himself! Please grant me that gospel-affirming, paradigm-shifting perspective that you are at work in my life by your sovereign grace, not merely in what is obviously good, but in what seems, at this moment, irredeemably bad. Grant me the trust to rejoice in my affliction as did Paul, who had the same indwelling Holy Spirit you've given to me.

37

Bitter Ingredients, Good Outcome

Even when I am old and gray,
    do not forsake me, O God,
till I declare your power to the next generation,
    your might to all who are to come.
Your righteousness reaches to the skies, O God,
    you who have done great things.
    Who, O God, is like you?
Though you have made me see troubles, many and bitter,
    you will restore my life again;
from the depths of the earth
    you will again bring me up.
You will increase my honor
    and comfort me once again.
I will praise you with the harp
    for your faithfulness, O my God;
I will sing praise to you with the lyre,
    O Holy One of Israel.

My lips will shout for joy
    when I sing praise to you—
    I, whom you have redeemed.

—PSALM 71:18–23

Like many psalms, this one contains both complaint and praise. The unknown psalmist speaks on behalf of God's people of all times, declaring that God has done great things while honestly affirming, "You have made me see troubles, many and bitter." Notice he recognizes not merely that bad things have happened but that his good God has had a hand in them.

No sooner does God's child say this than he declares his confidence that his destiny lies not in his many bitter troubles, but in God's sovereign and gracious plan for him: "You will restore my life again; from the depths of the earth you will again bring me up. You will increase my honor and comfort me once again."

He knows that as surely as God is God, his Redeemer will not forsake him. For the God of purpose has written a grand story, and the final glorious chapter, one that will never end, has not yet been acted out on Earth's stage.

Psalm 71 joins countless Scriptures in assuming the truth revealed in Romans 8:28—that God will, in the end, bring a magnificent outcome to what now, at times, seems dismally bitter.

There is an all-inclusiveness in the "all things" of Romans 8:28. No translation says each thing by itself *is* good, but that all things work together *for* good, and not on their own but under God's sovereign hand. Romans 8:28 declares a cumulative and ultimate good, not an individual or immediate good.

Before my mother would make a cake, she used to lay the ingredients on the kitchen counter. One day I decided to experiment. I tasted the individual ingredients for a chocolate cake. Baking powder. Baking soda. Raw eggs. Vanilla extract. I discovered that *almost everything that goes into a cake tastes terrible by itself.* But a remarkable metamorphosis took place when my mother mixed the ingredients in the right amounts and baked them together. The cake tasted delicious. Yet judging by the taste of each component, I never would have believed cake could taste so good.

In a similar way, the individual ingredients of trials and apparent tragedies taste bitter to us. Romans 8:28 doesn't tell me I should say, "It is good," if my leg breaks or my house burns down or I am robbed and beaten or my child dies. But no matter how bitter the taste of the individual components, God can carefully measure out and mix all ingredients together and regulate the temperature in order to produce a wonderful final product.

When Paul says, "for the good," he clearly implies final or ultimate good, not good subjectively felt in the midst of our sufferings. As his wife, Joy, underwent cancer treatments, C. S. Lewis wrote to a friend, "We are not necessarily doubting that God will do the best for us; we are wondering how painful the best will turn out to be."[28]

Father, the psalmist and Lewis didn't deny the painfulness and bitterness we must swallow in this fallen world. Neither

do we. But with them we affirm both your power and your commitment to us, your children, to do what will ultimately be best for us. Despite the repulsive flavor of some of its ingredients, give us a foretaste of that delicious chocolate cake you have promised. Thank you that though we could never turn the bad into good, you can, you do, and you will. It is why you are called the Redeemer.

38

Truly Triumphant over Evil

But if it is preached that Christ has been raised from the dead, how can some of you say that there is no resurrection of the dead? If there is no resurrection of the dead, then not even Christ has been raised. And if Christ has not been raised, our preaching is useless and so is your faith.... You are still in your sins. Then those also who have fallen asleep in Christ are lost. If only for this life we have hope in Christ, we are to be pitied more than all men.

But Christ has indeed been raised from the dead, the firstfruits of those who have fallen asleep. For since death came through a man, the resurrection of the dead comes also through a man. For as in Adam all die, so in Christ all will be made alive. But each in his own turn: Christ, the firstfruits; then, when he comes, those who belong to him. Then the end will come, when he hands over the kingdom to God the Father after he has destroyed all dominion, authority and power. For he must reign until he has put all his enemies under his feet. The last enemy to be destroyed is death.

—1 Corinthians 15:12–14, 17–26

God's redemptive plan will culminate in the resurrection of his children, in which he will once and for all conquer death and bring into being a refashioned universe, throbbing with vibrant, joyous eternal life. The promise of resurrection is what overshadows all present evil and suffering and assures its definitive end. Resurrection, and what it means to live forever in the presence of our God, is—or should be—what we live for.

Sadly, many people believe this life is all there is: "You only go around once on this Earth, so grab for whatever you can." But if you're a child of God, then you do *not* just "go around once"; you'll inhabit the New Earth forever! It's those in Hell who go around only once on Earth.

Here, we have bodies and we work, rest, play, and relate to one another—we call this *life*. Yet many have mistakenly redefined *eternal life* to mean a disembodied off-Earth existence stripped of human life's defining properties. In fact, eternal life will mean enjoying forever, as resurrected (which means embodied) beings, what life on Earth at its finest offered us. We could more accurately call our present existence the *beforelife* rather than calling Heaven the *afterlife*. Life doesn't merely continue in Heaven; it emerges at last to its intended fullness.

Dinesh D'Souza writes:

> The only way for us to really triumph over evil and suffering is to live forever in a place where those things do not exist. It is the claim of Christianity that there is such a place and that it is available to all who seek it.... If this claim is true, then evil and suffering...are as transient as our brief, mortal lives. In that case God has shown us a way to prevail over evil and suffering, which are finally overcome in the life to come.[29]

The resurrection means that the best parts about this world will carry over to the next, with none of the bad; hence, what we forgo here will prove no great loss. Only the resurrection can solve the gigantic problems of this world—and resurrection cannot come without death.

Without this eternal perspective, we assume that people who die young, who have handicaps, who suffer poor health, who don't get married or have children, or who don't do this or that will miss out on the best life has to offer. But the theology underlying those assumptions presumes that our present Earth, bodies, culture, relationships, and lives are all there is—or that they will somehow overshadow or negate those of the New Earth.

What are we thinking?

The stronger our concept of God and Heaven, the more we understand how Heaven will bring far more than compensation for our present sufferings.

God, overwhelm us with the far-reaching promises of resurrection. Help us live each day in anticipation of the life that awaits us on a brand-new Earth where we will live our lives in your presence, with your people and ours. Thank you for the place you are preparing for us now. Deliver us from the shortsighted unbelief that sees this world only as it is now, rather than as it will be one day because of your shed blood.

39

Suffering and the Glory to Come

The Spirit himself testifies with our spirit that we are God's children. Now if we are children, then we are heirs—heirs of God and co-heirs with Christ, if indeed we share in his sufferings in order that we may also share in his glory.

I consider that our present sufferings are not worth comparing with the glory that will be revealed in us. The creation waits in eager expectation for the sons of God to be revealed. For the creation was subjected to frustration, not by its own choice, but by the will of the one who subjected it, in hope that the creation itself will be liberated from its bondage to decay and brought into the glorious freedom of the children of God.

—ROMANS 8:16–21

God is preparing his children for a job—ruling a redeemed Earth. We've all seen what happens to princes and princesses raised in palaces, handed everything they want, having everything their way. They become spoiled and uncaring, poisoned by a spirit of entitlement. They aren't fit to be servant leaders but only tyrants. God is using our present school of adversity to prepare us to reign with Christ, the Servant King of servant kings.

When the New Testament discusses suffering, it repeatedly puts Heaven before the eyes of believers. Romans 8 tells us we'll become Christ's kingdom heirs and share in his glory *if* we share in his sufferings. No suffering, no glory.

F. F. Bruce writes, "It is not merely that the glory is a compensation for the suffering; it actually grows out of the suffering. There is an organic relation between the two for the believer as surely as there was for his Lord."[30]

Paul's one-word answer to the question, "Why suffering?" is *glory*. Glory is a state of high honor, involving a brilliant, radiant beauty. And God will be glorified by imparting his honor to us and sharing it with us.

God's promise of glory doesn't minimize our suffering, of course; Paul affirms in Romans 8 that we'll experience great sufferings. Only an immeasurably greater glory can eclipse our present suffering—and that is exactly what will happen. Romans 8:18 says God will not *create* that glory but will *reveal* it. It's already there—just not yet manifest.

My insulin-dependent diabetes has caused both my body and my mind to fail me. I suffer under the Curse enough to know just what I want—a new body and a new mind, a transformed heart without sin, suffering, or disability. Every passing year increases my longing to live on the resurrected Earth in my resurrected body with my resurrected family and friends, worshiping and serving the resurrected Jesus. I get goose bumps just thinking about it!

The treasures we'll enjoy won't lie only outside us, but as Paul says, "in us." God uses suffering to achieve the glorious transformation of our characters to prepare us for service and joy in the next life (see 2 Corinthians 4:17–18).

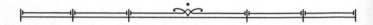

Father, thank you for preparing me for the family business— having dominion over creation and ruling Earth to your glory. That preparation is sometimes very difficult. Help me look forward to graduation, not only the event, but also the meaning of the event—that I will have been faithfully prepared by you to be a servant leader in your redeemed universe.

40

Ultimate Victory

And He who sits on the throne said, "Behold, I am making all things new." And He said, "Write, for these words are faithful and true." Then He said to me, "It is done. I am the Alpha and the Omega, the beginning and the end. I will give to the one who thirsts from the spring of the water of life without cost. He who overcomes will inherit these things, and I will be his God and he will be My son."

—REVELATION 21:5–7, NASB

Christ spoke these words after promising he would bring down Heaven itself to a New Earth, where God would forever dwell with his people. The incarnation of God's Son is eternal, and his throne and central dwelling place will be with us in that new world.

When Christ healed people on Earth, he knew that even they would one day grow weak again and die, leaving their families wailing over their graves. What could Jesus say to offer them hope not just for the short term but the long term? Luke tells us:

Blessed are you who are poor, for *yours is the kingdom of God.*
Blessed are you who hunger now, for *you will be satisfied.*
Blessed are you who weep now, for *you will laugh.* Blessed are
you when men hate you, when they exclude you and insult
you and reject your name as evil, because of the Son of Man.
Rejoice in that day and leap for joy, because *great is your
reward in heaven.* (Luke 6:20–23)

God will not simply wait for our deaths, then snap his fingers to
make us what he wants us to be. He begins that process here and now,
using our suffering to help us grow in Christlikeness. In *The Lord of
the Rings,* after the Dark Lord's ring of power is finally destroyed, Sam
asks Gandalf:

"Is everything sad going to come untrue? What's happened to
the world?"

"A great Shadow has departed," said Gandalf, and then he
laughed, and the sound was like music, or like water in a
parched land; and as he listened the thought came to [Sam]
that he had not heard laughter, the pure sound of merriment,
for days upon days without count.... It fell upon his ears like
the echo of all the joys he had ever known. But he himself
burst into tears. Then, as a sweet rain will pass down a wind of
spring and the sun will shine out the clearer, his tears ceased,
and his laughter welled up, and laughing he sprang from his
bed.

"How do I feel?" he cried. "Well, I don't know how to say
it. I feel, I feel"—he waved his arms in the air—"I feel like

spring after winter, and sun on the leaves; and like trumpets and harps and all the songs I have ever heard!"[31]

We can rejoice now because Jesus promises that in Heaven the hungry will find satisfaction. He assures those with eyes swollen from tears that they will laugh. He tells the persecuted to leap for joy *now* because of their great reward *then*.

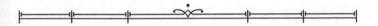

Thank you for the promise, Lord, that you haven't given up on this, your fallen creation. Thank you for having a plan in which you will renew Earth so we might forever enjoy it and have dominion over it for your glory. We treasure your promise of one day removing the great shadow and that in that day, and all the days after, we will laugh. We long to laugh as we delight in your presence, to laugh with each other, and to laugh with our risen Jesus, who created laughter and promises it as part of the coming new world. Bring laughter to us this day, and help us see it as your delight-drenched foretaste of eternal life.

41

No More Curse

So will it be with the resurrection of the dead. The body that is sown is perishable, it is raised imperishable; it is sown in dishonor, it is raised in glory; it is sown in weakness, it is raised in power; it is sown a natural body, it is raised a spiritual body.

If there is a natural body, there is also a spiritual body. So it is written: "The first man Adam became a living being"; the last Adam, a life-giving spirit. The spiritual did not come first, but the natural, and after that the spiritual. The first man was of the dust of the earth, the second man from heaven. As was the earthly man, so are those who are of the earth; and as is the man from heaven, so also are those who are of heaven. And just as we have borne the likeness of the earthly man, so shall we bear the likeness of the man from heaven.

—1 CORINTHIANS 15:42–49

God's children live now in the perishable, awaiting the imperishable. We live in temporary dishonor preceding eternal honor.

We live in the fallen but are destined for the risen. Around the corner, resurrection awaits us.

Many people look to cosmetic surgeries and other techniques to renovate crumbling bodies. We try to hold on to youthfulness with a white-knuckled grip, but all in vain.

Due to my disease, I have lain helpless, stiff as a board, not in my right mind, needing my wife to get sugar in my mouth. My once-strong body grows weak. Low blood sugar clouds my judgment and leaves me with a memory of having said stupid things, like a drunken man. Several times a year I have severe reactions in which I don't know what's happening to me.

This humbles me. But I can honestly say I am grateful for it; yes, I even *delight* in it because I recognize the value of being humbled, for "when I am weak, then I am strong" (2 Corinthians 12:10). My weakness drives me to greater dependence upon Christ. I wouldn't begin to trade the spiritual benefits I've received.

The God who rules the world with truth and grace won't feel satisfied until he removes every sin, sorrow, and thorn. If redemption failed to reach the farthest boundaries of the Curse, it would remain incomplete. The Curse is real but *temporary*. Jesus will reverse the Curse.

If the present Earth under the Curse can seem so beautiful and wonderful, if our bodies, so weakened by the Curse, at times feel overcome with a sense of the Earth's majesty and splendor—then *how magnificent will the New Earth be?* And what will it feel like to enjoy it in perfect bodies? God promises that every one of his children will one day experience the answers to those questions.

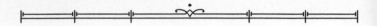

Father, help us to believe in the coming resurrection not merely as an ancient doctrine but as a warm and personal and living promise, obtained for us by your extravagant love and almighty power. Help us not merely to affirm the resurrection but to embrace its true meaning, to be captivated by it in our imaginations, and to live today in light of the eternal joy of your resurrected people, exalting the resurrected Christ on a resurrected Earth.

42

The Best Is Yet to Come

For we know in part and we prophesy in part; but when the perfect comes, the partial will be done away. When I was a child, I used to speak like a child, think like a child, reason like a child; when I became a man, I did away with childish things. For now we see in a mirror dimly, but then face to face; now I know in part, but then I will know fully just as I also have been fully known. But now faith, hope, love, abide these three; but the greatest of these is love.

—1 CORINTHIANS 13:9–13, NASB

To see now in a mirror dimly is to catch a glimpse of reality but not perceive its full features. We may fail to see what's really there and see instead what isn't. But what will it mean for us, in God's presence, to know fully?

Obviously, we won't know everything. Only God is omniscient, and after we die we will still be finite creatures, not infinite. But at the very least, to know fully will involve remembering accurately.

When Christ sets up his eternal kingdom, he will banish evil and suffering—yet we will remember both in a way that won't cause us pain but will prompt our gratitude and worship. God told the Israelites to remember their bondage in Egypt, long after he had freed them, as they celebrated Passover each year (see Exodus 12:14). Likewise, I'm convinced that in Heaven we'll remember evil and suffering in order to provide the backdrop to better see God's holiness and grace.

Heaven's happiness won't be dependent on our ignorance of what happened on Earth; it will be enhanced by our changed *perspective* on it. We'll remember the sufferings of the present in order to appreciate our eternal future.

My friend Jim Harrell, while dying of ALS, wrote me, "I hope I never lose the memory of this illness throughout eternity. Keeping the memory will help me worship Jesus in a much deeper way. Also, having the memory of my paralysis will make each day, each breath, and each movement more enjoyable and more fulfilling." We'll enjoy the magnificence of our God and his Heaven not merely *in spite of* all we suffered here; we'll enjoy it all the more *because of* everything we suffered here.

Failing to grasp God's promises concerning the world to come sets us up for both discouragement and sin. We tell ourselves, *If I don't experience an intimate friendship now, I never will.* Or, *If I can't afford to travel to that beautiful place now, I never will.* We feel desperate to get what we *think* we want. So we're tempted toward fornication, indebtedness, or theft.

But if we understand both the negative truth that God will judge all sin and the positive truth that we'll actually live in a new universe full of new opportunities, then we can forego certain pleasures and experiences *now,* knowing we can enjoy far greater ones *later.*

A moment after we die physically, a dramatic upward movement will take us immediately to Christ. We'll go right on living, just in another place. And one day, in the resurrection, we'll live again on Earth, a life so rich and joyful as to make this life seem utterly impoverished. Millions of years from now, we'll still look, feel, and *be* young.

As we live in God's redeemed universe, we should expect our knowledge, skills, and life experiences to continue to develop. So don't ever think that because your body and mind are now no longer at their best that you have passed your peak. If you are God's child, then the resurrection of your body and mind awaits, as does eternal life on the New Earth. Don't worry—you will *never* pass your peak! The best is yet to come!

Father, help us understand that these words are not mere positive thinking but are firmly rooted in your own promises, which you have not made lightly. The weight of your infinite being is behind and beneath the promise of resurrection and everlasting pleasures in the land of our Master's joy. Help us see our losses of physical and mental sharpness not as permanent but merely temporary. Because of Christ's redemptive work, in the resurrection we won't simply return to better health; we'll move forward to minds and bodies untainted by sin—better by far than what we've ever known.

43

Forever Healed and Whole

I will exalt you, O LORD,
>   for you lifted me out of the depths
>   and did not let my enemies gloat over me.
O LORD my God, I called to you for help
>   and you healed me.
O LORD, you brought me up from the grave;
>   you spared me from going down into the pit.
Sing to the LORD, you saints of his;
>   praise his holy name.
For his anger lasts only a moment,
>   but his favor lasts a lifetime;
weeping may remain for a night,
>   but rejoicing comes in the morning.

>   —PSALM 30:1–5

God's people can sing his praises, for while we may weep for a night, we have his promise of unabated rejoicing in the eternal morning awaiting us.

I had the privilege of spending two hours alone with Campus Crusade founder Bill Bright six months before he died. As Bill sat there, tubes running from his oxygen tank into his nostrils, he almost jumped out of his chair as we talked about Heaven and the God he loved.

Bill Bright reminded me of those who "saw [the things promised] and welcomed them from a distance" and "admitted that they were aliens and strangers on earth," because "they are looking for a country of their own" and "they were longing for a better country—a heavenly one." We're told of these people, "Therefore God is not ashamed to be called their God, for he has prepared a city for them" (Hebrews 11:13–16).

We don't have to just admire such people. By God's grace, we can *be* such people!

The wonders of our resurrected bodies and our future lives on the New Earth await us. But as we enjoy them, day after day, surely we'll look back to this life with profound gratitude for how God used everything, even evil and suffering, to prepare us for our eternal home.

You may not feel satisfied with your current body or mind, but your resurrection upgrade will never disappoint you.

Over the years, Joni Eareckson Tada has become a dear friend of ours. Joni says:

I still can hardly believe it. I, with shriveled, bent fingers, atrophied muscles, gnarled knees, and no feeling from the shoulders down, will one day have a new body, light, bright, and clothed in righteousness—powerful and dazzling. Can you imagine the hope this gives someone spinal cord–injured like me? Or someone who is cerebral palsied, brain-injured, or who has multiple sclerosis? Imagine the hope this gives someone who is manic-depressive. No other religion, no other philosophy promises new bodies, hearts, and minds. Only in the Gospel of Christ do hurting people find such incredible hope.[32]

Joni once spoke to a class of mentally handicapped Christians. They smiled when she said that one day she would get a new body. But then she added, "And *you're* going to get new minds." The class erupted in cheers and applause. They knew what they most looked forward to!

Our resurrected bodies will fulfill their highest function as we glorify God, worshiping him without hindrance, fatigue, or distraction. Many disabled believers have heard others say about the resurrection, "You must look forward to walking and running." True enough, but one handicapped Christian made a particularly revealing comment: "What I look forward to most is kneeling."

Lord, while this life's tide moves us back and forth from weeping to rejoicing, thank you for giving us something to look forward to: a world where you promise to wipe away each and every tear from your children's eyes. With people like Bill Bright and Joni Tada as our examples, we celebrate the truth that in the coming eternal morning, we will no longer suffer but will forever experience joyful pleasures at your right hand. Thank you for purchasing by your suffering all of our joys, both here and in the world to come.

44

Forever Joyful

As the rain and the snow
    come down from heaven,
and do not return to it without watering the earth
and making it bud and flourish,
    so that it yields seed for the sower and bread for the eater,
so is my word that goes out from my mouth:
    It will not return to me empty,
but will accomplish what I desire
    and achieve the purpose for which I sent it.
You will go out in joy and be led forth in peace;
the mountains and hills
    will burst into song before you,
and all the trees of the fieldwill clap their hands.
Instead of the thornbush will grow the pine tree,
    and instead of briers the myrtle will grow.
This will be for the LORD's renown,
    for an everlasting sign,
    which will not be destroyed.

—ISAIAH 55:10–13

One day God's children will enter joyfully into a renewed Earth, being led forth in peace, watching and listening in slack-jawed, bright-eyed wonder as the mountains and hills burst into song before us. Celebrating the creative wonder of the Redeemer's new world, even the trees of the field will applaud thunderously. The entire creation that now groans will break free and join in the greatest party in the history of the universe.

As a teenager held in a Japanese prison camp in China, Margaret Holder felt the almost unbearable pain of forced separation from her family. But as the war progressed, American planes dropped barrels of food and supplies. When Nanci and I spoke with her forty-five years later, Margaret recalled with delight "care packages falling from the sky."

One day an American plane flew low and dropped more of those wonderful food barrels. But as the barrels neared the ground, the captives realized something had changed. Her eyes bright, Margaret told us, "This time the barrels had legs!" The sky rained American soldiers, parachuting down to rescue them. Margaret and several hundred children rushed out of the camp past the Japanese guards, who offered no resistance. Free for the first time in six years, they ran to the soldiers, throwing themselves on their rescuers, hugging and kissing them.

Imagine the children's joy! Imagine the soldiers' joy!

Yes, I realize that those six years of confinement and separation from family caused great suffering for that young girl and her family. But I also know what I saw in the eyes and heard in the voice of Margaret Holder almost half a century later. She exuded sheer *joy,* a joy she never would have known without the suffering that preceded it. In the decades since their dramatic rescue from that prison camp, most of those children have died. Those who loved Jesus are now with him. Imagine their joy in being reunited *yet again* with their parents and with some of their rescuers! But this time the reunion will never end. And this time they will live forever with Jesus, the source of all joy.

If the soldiers rejoiced in rescuing those children, think how God rejoices in rescuing us. Whether he returns in the sky to liberate us or draws us to himself through our deaths, he will indeed rescue us and unite us with him and our loved ones who know him. He'll liberate us from a world under the Curse and take us home to the place where mountains and hills break into song and the trees clap their hands.

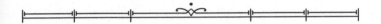

Thank you, Father, for the deliverance you've promised. We rejoice that all creation waits in eager expectation for our revelation as resurrected rulers of a New Earth. As the creation fell on our coattails, it will rise on our coattails. Our resurrection, at long last, will release this fallen world from its bondage. What a day that will be when all your people, and the world you made us to govern, will unite in unbridled praise to you.

45

The Shadow of Hell

There is nothing concealed that will not be disclosed, or hidden that will not be made known. What I tell you in the dark, speak in the daylight; what is whispered in your ear, proclaim from the roofs. Do not be afraid of those who kill the body but cannot kill the soul. Rather, be afraid of the One who can destroy both soul and body in hell. Are not two sparrows sold for a penny? Yet not one of them will fall to the ground apart from the will of your Father. And even the very hairs of your head are all numbered. So don't be afraid; you are worth more than many sparrows.

Whoever acknowledges me before men, I will also acknowledge him before my Father in heaven. But whoever disowns me before men, I will disown him before my Father in heaven.

—MATTHEW 10:26–33

Jesus tells us that if we fear God, we need not fear anyone or anything else. God knows all, never relinquishes control, and brings judgment upon evildoers. He considers his children precious. He calls upon us to trust him and acknowledge him before others.

Do you long for a world in which evil and corruption don't exist? Then you long for a Heaven without evildoers. And that requires God to either force everyone to repent and embrace Christ's righteousness or provide an alternative residence for those who don't. Hell is that place.

Hell is not evil; it is a place where evil is punished. Hell is not pleasant, appealing, or encouraging. But Hell is morally good because a good God must punish evil.

The best reason for believing in Hell is that Jesus said it exists. Jesus taught that an unbridgeable chasm separates the wicked in Hell from the righteous in Paradise. To fear and dread Hell is understandable, but to argue against Hell is to argue against justice. If there is no Hell, there is no justice. Life in this fallen world will give way to an unending life, either in Heaven or Hell. *That* life, not this one, will bring perfect justice.

Just as most people in prison don't think they belong there, so most of us can't imagine we deserve Hell. But when at last we begin to grasp that we do deserve it, we can then praise God for his grace on a far deeper level.

Heaven and Hell are places defined, respectively, by God's presence or absence, by God's grace or wrath. They're real places but also conditions of relationship to God. Whose we are, not where we are, determines our misery or our joy.

For the Hell-bound, suffering can serve as a frightening foretaste of Hell. Suffering reminds us of our imminent death, the wages for our sin. In our suffering we should look at our own evils and failures and beg God for mercy. If we reject the best gift that a holy and gracious God can offer us, purchased with his own blood, what remains, in the end, will be nothing but Hell.

C. S. Lewis wrote:

> In the long run the answer to all those who object to the
> doctrine of hell is itself a question: "What are you asking God
> to do?" To wipe out their past sins and, at all costs, to give
> them a fresh start, smoothing every difficulty and offering
> every miraculous help? But He has done so, on Calvary. To
> forgive them? They will not be forgiven. To leave them alone?
> Alas, I am afraid that is what He does.[33]

The sufferings of the present are a bittersweet reminder of the horrors of Hell, from which God has—in his sacrificial love for us—delivered us.

Earth under the Curse is an in-between world touched by both Heaven and Hell. Our lives here lead directly into Heaven or directly into Hell, affording a choice between the two. The best of life on Earth is a glimpse of Heaven; the worst of life on Earth is a glimpse of Hell. For Christians, this present life is the closest they will come to Hell. For unbelievers, it is the closest they will come to Heaven.

Father, we live in a world that considers Hell a barbaric
concept. Help us to believe that you know better than the
world. When we imagine we don't deserve Hell, we flatter

ourselves as being far better than we are. If we understood your holiness even for a moment, we would no longer be amazed that you would send sinners to Hell. Rather, we'd be amazed that you took Hell on yourself in order to transform sinful rebels into righteous children and open to us the doors of Heaven.

46

How Much Is Too Much?

Blessed be the God and Father of our Lord Jesus Christ, the Father of mercies and God of all comfort, who comforts us in all our affliction, so that we may be able to comfort those who are in any affliction, with the comfort with which we ourselves are comforted by God. For as we share abundantly in Christ's sufferings, so through Christ we share abundantly in comfort too. If we are afflicted, it is for your comfort and salvation; and if we are comforted, it is for your comfort, which you experience when you patiently endure the same sufferings that we suffer. Our hope for you is unshaken, for we know that as you share in our sufferings, you will also share in our comfort.

—2 CORINTHIANS 1:3–7, ESV

God patiently withholds his judgment to extend us grace. While that delay requires the delay of Christ's return and postpones relief of suffering in this fallen world, it also gives far more people the opportunity to enter the world, become God's children, serve him, grow in Christlikeness, bring him glory, and ultimately enjoy eternal life.

Without this bigger picture, ongoing suffering over centuries and millennia certainly seems excessive. But suppose God permitted evil and suffering, yet limited us to one ghastly year of human history. Would we consider that duration of evil and suffering acceptable? What if someone could prove that we would become greater and happier beings for all eternity as a result, would you think it right for God to allow ten seconds of intense suffering? Likely you would.

But if we could justify ten seconds of great suffering, then why not ten hours, ten days, or ten years? And in eternity how much longer will ninety years seem than ninety minutes?

So how much evil and suffering is too much? Rate all pain on a scale of one to ten, with ten representing "engulfed in flames" and "mild sunburn" earning a one. If God eliminated level-ten pain, then level-nine pain would become the worst. God could reduce the worst suffering to level three, but then level three would seem unbearable. If we judge God's goodness strictly by his elimination of pain, in the end, we will not be satisfied if he permits any pain at all.

Often when we suffer, we think only of receiving comfort, not giving it. But when God brings us affliction and then comforts us, we are enabled to use that same comfort to console others. We become God's representatives to the hurting. It's fulfilling to be God's instruments, and that's a source of comfort as well. When we see how we've helped others, we witness yet another purpose for our own suffering.

I frequently receive letters from those whose loved ones have died. One man wrote, "We lost our three little girls in an airplane accident ten months ago.... My wife and I decided to pursue God through this tragedy. We had to choose life or death, and God has been faithful to comfort and change our lives from the inside out. After suffering this loss, we know that the only important things now are the ones that will last for eternity."

First Corinthians 12:26 speaks of the body of Christ: "If one part suffers, every part suffers." Sometimes God wraps his arms around us in the form of another person.

To say that God takes too long to bring final judgment on evil and suffering imposes an artificial timetable on someone time cannot contain. God's Son entered time in his incarnation. Though he understands our impatience, he won't yield to it—and I'm convinced that one day we, and those we've been able to help because of what we've been through, will be grateful he didn't.

We want suffering to end now, Lord. Not tomorrow but today. And yet we are the beneficiaries of your wisdom and grace in delaying justice and extending mercy, even at the cost of continued suffering. Thank you that you are not only merciful but all-wise, and you know the right time for each of us to leave this world and the right time for you to return to set up your kingdom and swallow up death forever. Come, Lord Jesus—but come at the time you know to be best.

47

God's Unseen Intervention

Can a mother forget the baby at her breast
and have no compassion on the child she has borne?
Though she may forget,
I will not forget you!
See, I have engraved you on the palms of my hands;
your walls are ever before me.

— ISAIAH 49:15–16

Though I can't prove it, I'm convinced God prevents far more evil than he allows. When his people are discouraged, God says that he can no more forget us and fail to have compassion than a mother could fail her own child. In fact, though some mothers have failed their children, God will never fail us. "See, I have engraved you on the palms of my hands." What a powerful statement—by his own doing, we are permanently fixed on the very hands of God! And knowing us and loving us as he does, he often intervenes in ways we don't always recognize.

On January 15, 2009, what should have brought certain death to passengers aboard US Airways Flight 1549, and catastrophe to Manhattan, turned into what secular reporters labeled a "miracle." The pilot, Chesley Sullenberger, safely landed a crippled plane in New York's Hudson River, with no serious injuries.

While chunks of ice and busy ferries filled most of the river, the place where the plane came down remained clear of both ice and boats. It landed without breaking apart. Ferryboat captains rescued all 155 people from the frigid river within minutes.[34]

Though the miracle of Flight 1549 appears to be the exception, not the rule, isn't it likely that a kind, all-powerful, and very compassionate God routinely prevents terrible tragedies in ways that we do not see and therefore do not credit as miracles? Perhaps one day we'll hear those stories and marvel at how often God intervened when we imagined him uninvolved in our world.

Focusing on God's big miracles—like curing cancer and making brain tumors disappear—causes us to overlook his "small" daily miracles of providence in which he holds the universe together, provides us with air to breathe and lungs to breathe it, food to eat and stomachs to digest it. Our birthright does not include pain-free living. Only those who understand that this world languishes under the Curse will marvel at the beauties he provides us despite that Curse.

Lord, there's so much to be grateful for. Thanks for watching over us. We have no basis for believing that we as fallen

*creatures deserve a better world, and every basis to believe
we deserve a worse one. Yet in your grace, you have guaran-
teed in Christ that we will live in such a world forever. Our
thanks don't seem adequate, but thank you nonetheless.*

48

Grateful for the Wait

But do not forget this one thing, dear friends: With the Lord a day is like a thousand years, and a thousand years are like a day. The Lord is not slow in keeping his promise, as some understand slowness. He is patient with you, not wanting anyone to perish, but everyone to come to repentance.

— 2 PETER 3:8-9

For many, the most difficult problem with evil is its persistence. God "has set a day when he will judge the world with justice" (Acts 17:31). But why a *future* day of judgment?

Barbara Brown Taylor phrased it, "What kind of God allows the innocent to suffer while the wicked pop their champagne corks and sing loud songs?"[35]

We may say, "Yes, Lord, we accept your wisdom in permitting evil and suffering for a season—but enough is enough. *Why do you let it continue?*"

The Bible echoes the same sentiment. Jeremiah said, "You are always righteous, O LORD, when I bring a case before you. Yet I would speak with you about your justice: Why does the way of the wicked prosper? Why do all the faithless live at ease?" (12:1).

Why doesn't God simply reward each good and punish each evil as it happens? Because God's justice is not a vending machine in which a coin of righteousness immediately produces reward or a coin of evil yields swift retribution. Scripture assures us justice is coming. Everything in God's plan has a proper time; the gap between the present and that proper time tests and incubates our faith. When reward and punishment are immediate, no faith in God is required or cultivated.

The wheels of justice may seem to turn slowly, but they turn surely. Some rewards of goodness and punishments of evil come in this life. And though ultimate rewards and punishments await the final judgment, considerable justice—both reward and retribution—is dispensed upon death, when God's children immediately experience the joy of his presence and the unrepentant suffer the first justice of Hell (see Luke 16:19–31). This means that the maximum duration of injustice experienced by any person cannot exceed his life span.

Don't we give thanks for God's patience with Saul, the self-righteous killer who became Paul? Or John Newton, the evil slave trader who accepted God's amazing grace and wrote the song that countless millions have sung?

God drew me to himself in 1969. But what if Christ had answered the prayers of many in those days and had returned and brought final judgment in 1968? Or in 1953, the year before I was born? Where would I be for eternity? Where would you be?

I'm grateful God was patient enough with fallen humanity to allow the world to continue until I was created, and then continue further until I became part of his family.

Aren't you grateful for the same? If God answered our prayers to return today, who might be lost that he plans to save tomorrow?

Lord, you are the potter; we are the clay. You have the right to do what you choose. But if we look carefully at what you choose, we may see wisdom and purpose and mercy even in what we don't fully understand. Thanks for not answering the prayers for Christ's immediate return offered by the generations that preceded me and my family. I'd hate to think of us not existing, of not being able to love you and serve you and glorify you forever.

49

Surrendering to God's Wisdom

The LORD said to Job:

"Will the one who contends with the Almighty correct him?

Let him who accuses God answer him!"

Then Job answered the LORD:

"I am unworthy—how can I reply to you?

I put my hand over my mouth.

I spoke once, but I have no answer—

twice, but I will say no more."

Then the LORD spoke to Job out of the storm:

"Brace yourself like a man;

I will question you,

and you shall answer me.

Would you discredit my justice?

Would you condemn me to justify yourself?

Do you have an arm like God's,

and can your voice thunder like his?"

—JOB 40:1–9

When I need a point-of-view adjustment, I read the last five chapters of Job. That's where the focus shifts from Job's questions about his suffering—and his friends' proposed answers—to God's majesty. Job had a better basis for complaint than nearly any of us ever will. Yet after listening to Job's grievances, God finally speaks to him: "Brace yourself like a man; I will question you, and you shall answer me" (Job 38:3).

God is saying, "You are unhappy with me, Job. You have questioned me. You assume you know far more than you do. Now it's my turn to ask you some questions." God never faults Job for being finite, only for failing to recognize that he has no right to pass judgment on the wisdom and goodness of an infinite Creator.

"Where were you when I laid the earth's foundation? Tell me, if you understand. Who marked off its dimensions? Surely you know!" (verses 4–5).

God has always been; Job just showed up. In Hebrew culture, wisdom came with old age. God is eternally old, Job ridiculously young.

God says, "Tell me, if you understand." Job doesn't and can't.

We lack God's omniscience, omnipotence, wisdom, holiness, justice, and goodness. If we insist we have the right, or even assume we have the capacity, to understand the hidden purposes of God, we forfeit the comfort and perspective we could have had in kneeling before his vastly superior wisdom.

While this doesn't answer the question of evil and suffering, it does suggest God's answer is beyond our understanding. One day we'll know far better than now; but even in eternity, God will still be infinite, and we'll still be finite.

Job finally says to God, "Surely I spoke of things I did not understand, things too wonderful for me to know.... My ears had heard of you but now my eyes have seen you. Therefore I despise myself and repent in dust and ashes" (42:3, 5–6).

Charles Spurgeon stated, "He who demands a reason from God is not in a fit state to receive one."[36] It is when Job surrenders himself to God that he at last, at the end of himself, finds comfort.

Father, thank you for both inviting us to ask questions and instructing us to listen carefully to your answers. Help us rely on you even when we don't understand. As a loving Father, you want us to trust you rather than blame and resent you. After all you've done for us as Creator and Redeemer, how could we do less?

50

Too Small to See the Big Picture

Seek the LORD while he may be found;
    call on him while he is near.
Let the wicked forsake his way
    and the evil man his thoughts.
Let him turn to the LORD, and he will have mercy on him,
    and to our God, for he will freely pardon.
"For my thoughts are not your thoughts,
    neither are your ways my ways," declares the LORD.
"As the heavens are higher than the earth,
    so are my ways higher than your ways
    and my thoughts than your thoughts."

—ISAIAH 55:6–9

Why should I, a finite and fallen creature, expect that I will understand God's reasons for doing what he does and allowing what he allows? If God always thought the way I do, something would be terribly wrong with him.

I can't say that a commensurate good has yet come out of every bad situation my loved ones and I have experienced. But I can say I have seen *great* and surpassing good come out of some of them. And I have also seen *some* good come through each of them, enough to give me faith that there may exist countless goods I cannot see. Since we know that happens *sometimes,* couldn't it happen far more often than we realize?

A few years ago, a friend told me about the deep and lasting impression the Willis family's tragedy had made on him when he saw their powerful interviews in 1994 as the story unfolded. Now, suppose God had appeared to Scott and Janet before their van exploded on the freeway, and said, "I'm about to take six of your children to Heaven, but I want to assure you that it will touch many people deeply and for many years." Would God's explanation have made their experience easier? I doubt it. Were God to explain why he permits us to experience each instance of suffering and evil, sometimes we might feel even worse. We're just too small to see the big picture.

We tend to see God as a bigger, smarter version of ourselves. We say, "A good man wouldn't allow all this evil if he could stop it." If we had the power, we say, we'd stop it; therefore, so should God. But God is *not* like us: "God is not a man, that he should lie, nor a son of man, that he should change his mind" (Numbers 23:19). God says, "You thought I was altogether like you" (Psalm 50:21). Whatever seems good to us, we think, should be good to God. Whatever we think is fair, God should do. We wouldn't permit murders and poverty, so neither should God.

Yet we have neither the qualifications nor the authority to exercise such judgment. Not only does God's character infinitely surpass our own, but his thoughts and perspectives radically transcend ours.

When a child falls off a bike, she doesn't need her father to say, "Sweetheart, here's why it happened—given your speed and the weight of this bike, it couldn't tolerate that sharp turn and..." No. The child simply wants comfort. We don't need explanations; we need "God, who comforts the downcast" (2 Corinthians 7:6). God doesn't always explain why we suffer, yet millions of people attest to the comfort he has brought them in their darkest hours.

God, in all my hardest times, you have been there. You've been faithful to me when I had to resign as a pastor, had issues with church leaders, went through lawsuits and public scorn, was restricted to minimum wage, and faced disease and depression and the deaths of close friends and family members. I don't understand why everything has happened, but I have seen a great deal of good come out of much of it. Because of who you are and all you've done for me, I trust you to use all the other difficulties in ways I will not understand until I enter your presence.

51

The Difference Between Pain and Suffering

For God does speak—now one way, now another—
    though man may not perceive it.
In a dream, in a vision of the night,
    when deep sleep falls on men
    as they slumber in their beds,
he may speak in their ears
    and terrify them with warnings,
to turn man from wrongdoing
    and keep him from pride,
to preserve his soul from the pit,
    his life from perishing by the sword.
Or a man may be chastened on a bed of pain
    with constant distress in his bones,
so that his very being finds food repulsive
    and his soul loathes the choicest meal.
His flesh wastes away to nothing,
    and his bones, once hidden, now stick out.

His soul draws near to the pit,
>
>> and his life to the messengers of death.
>
> Yet if there is an angel on his side
>
>> as a mediator, one out of a thousand,
>>
>> to tell a man what is right for him,
>
> to be gracious to him and say,
>
>> "Spare him from going down to the pit;
>>
>> I have found a ransom for him"—
>
> then his flesh is renewed like a child's;
>
>> it is restored as in the days of his youth.

—JOB 33:14–25

Job spoke about his pain with intense honesty. And God thought it worthy to include in the Bible. Based on the design of the human body, I believe God created pain for our own benefit. Even in Eden, before there was sin and death, limited and temporary pain could have served a good purpose, for instance in prompting Adam and Eve to pull their hands away from fire. That kind of pain is very different from *suffering*—relentless pain inflicted by people upon each other and the breakdown of body and mind that leads us toward death. *That* was the result of sin and the Curse.

Someone once asked Father Damien at his leper colony on Molokai, Hawaii, what gift he would pray for his patients to receive. Without pause, he answered, "Pain."

Leprosy prevents the body from feeling pain, with disastrous results. That's why leprosy specialist Dr. Paul Brand, with coauthor Philip Yancey, describes pain as an "ingenious invention."[37]

Leprosy, also called Hansen's disease, desensitizes nerve endings. The lack of pain allows the sufferer to do himself serious damage without realizing it. He might walk on a broken leg; she might leave her hands on a scalding pot. Without pain's warning system, we would either have to be made invulnerable to our environment or would have to be made inhuman in order to survive. Ironically, pain-lessness is one manifestation of the Curse.

As leprosy proves, bodies that can't feel pain are terribly deprived. Similarly, in this fallen world, if we felt no emotional pain, we would live as relational lepers, never understanding the harm we inflict upon others and ourselves. Without feeling the consequences of our evil and others' evil, we could not see our fallen nature and our desperate need for Christ's redemptive work.

We applaud Susanna Wesley, mother of Charles and John Wesley, as a great prayer warrior and mentor of her children. But remember, nine of her children died by age two. Even if we see the Curse or the devil as the reason for these deaths, God permitted and used her profound suffering to make her a champion of the faith.

The problem isn't the existence of pain, nor of brief and obviously purposeful suffering. The real problem is the extent and intensity of suffering, especially when we don't see its purpose. God uses pain to get our attention and dissipate the illusion that all is well.

Worse things can happen to us than dying young of a terrible disease. We could live in health and wealth. But to die without Christ and go to Hell—or to know Christ but fail to draw close to him—is immeasurably worse than the disease that gets our attention and prompts us to look to him.

Father, it seems limited pain may have had a purpose in a sinless world. But we know the suffering of this present world isn't what you had in mind for Eden or what we'll experience on the New Earth. Yet even now you can use crisis and suffering to get our attention, to help us reset our priorities, to direct us to you and banish the illusion that we can take care of ourselves. God, preserve us from the devil's lie that we don't need you. Use all means at your disposal, even those that hurt, to draw us closer to you and prompt us to live this brief life in light of eternity.

52

Suffering's Limits

For men are not cast off
    by the Lord forever.
Though he brings grief, he will show compassion,
    so great is his unfailing love.
For he does not willingly bring affliction
    or grief to the children of men.
To crush underfoot
    all prisoners in the land,
to deny a man his rights
    before the Most High,
to deprive a man of justice—
    would not the Lord see such things?
Who can speak and have it happen
    if the Lord has not decreed it?
Is it not from the mouth of the Most High
    that both calamities and good things come?
Why should any living man complain
    when punished for his sins?
Let us examine our ways and test them,
    and let us return to the LORD.

—LAMENTATIONS 3:31–40

I n this single passage, only verses apart, we're told God doesn't willingly bring affliction or grief, and we're told that both calamities and good things come from God. What can this mean?

Even though the statements seem contradictory, they are not. While God finds no pleasure in sending affliction or grief to us, and he empathizes with our suffering, he can and does accomplish good purposes in our lives through them.

One reason the problem of evil and suffering can seem so acute to us is the cumulative weight we feel from media oversaturation. At most, people used to bear the sufferings of their own families, communities, or nations. Now, through instant access to global events, we witness the sufferings of an entire world. While a tiny percentage of the world's inhabitants face a given crisis, the images each day of one disaster after another make it feel far more universal. This oversaturation desensitizes some to suffering while overwhelming others.

Despite the horror of disasters, we must understand that suffering does not have a cumulative nature. The terrible suffering of six million people may seem six million times worse than the suffering of one. But no one, except God, can experience the suffering of six million people. All of us remain limited to our own suffering. While our suffering may include an emotional burden for others who suffer, it cannot grow larger than we are. The limits of our finite beings dictate the limits of our suffering.

C. S. Lewis concluded, "There is no such thing as a sum of suffering, for no one suffers it. When we have reached the maximum that a single person can suffer, we have, no doubt, reached something very horrible, but we have reached all the suffering there ever can be in the universe. The addition of a million fellow-sufferers adds no more pain."[38]

Consider that while our suffering can rise only to the level we individually can suffer, Jesus suffered for all of us. All the evils and suffering that we tell him he never should have permitted, he willingly inflicted upon himself, for us.

Think about that long and hard, and let it pierce your heart with wonder and praise.

Lord, if we understood the extent of your empathy for us and the extent of your suffering to make us your children, we would surely be embarrassed to express our displeasure with you when your plans turn out to be radically different from ours. While we tend to live for the pursuit of our happiness, you are committed to the pursuit of our holiness. Teach us that when we pursue only happiness we will lose it along with holiness, but when we find holiness, including the holiness that can come to us through difficulties, we will find the happiness of Heaven.

53

Worshiping Through Our Tears

When the LORD brought back the captives to Zion,
    we were like men who dreamed.
Our mouths were filled with laughter,
    our tongues with songs of joy.
Then it was said among the nations,
    "The LORD has done great things for them."
The LORD has done great things for us,
    and we are filled with joy.
Restore our fortunes, O LORD,
    like streams in the Negev.
Those who sow in tears
    will reap with songs of joy.
He who goes out weeping,
    carrying seed to sow,
will return with songs of joy,
    carrying sheaves with him.

—PSALM 126

The psalmist rejoices in God's deliverance from captivity with a greater joy than he could ever have experienced had there been no captivity. This is the nature of joy—it is always greater and deeper for those who have known real sorrow. Notice the contrast: "Those who sow in tears will reap with songs of joy. He who goes out weeping…will return with songs of joy."

Adam and Eve knew joy in the garden, to be sure, but had they continued in innocence, they could never have realized some joy-awakening aspects of God's character—his grace, mercy, and patience among them. I don't mean the Fall was good—it was a horrid and tragic thing—nevertheless, God, in his redemptive plan, has brought and will bring great eternal good even out of that tragedy.

We should not be surprised, therefore, when God allows us to undergo sorrows that will forever deepen and broaden our worship of him and our experience of eternal joy.

But trusting Christ doesn't mean we suffer less. When my wife and I passed through a particularly difficult period of our lives, we felt like we'd "done our time," as if we shouldn't have to face more difficulty for a while. But that's not how it works. As everyone living with ongoing disabilities, diseases, and heartaches knows, in this life God does not parcel out a certain amount of suffering so once it runs out we'll face no more.

Nancy Guthrie's disabled daughter, Hope, died after living through 199 days of seizures and other complications. Nancy writes:

> The day after we buried Hope, my husband said to me, "You know, I think we expected our faith to make this hurt less, but it doesn't. Our faith gave us an incredible amount of strength

and encouragement while we had Hope, and we are comforted by the knowledge that she is in heaven. Our faith keeps
us from being swallowed by despair. But I don't think it
makes our loss hurt any less."[39]

Their pain didn't decrease because they believed; rather, their
faith kept their pain from incapacitating them. When I interviewed
David and Nancy Guthrie, they said God stood with them *in* their
pain, but God did not *remove* their pain. Nancy says:

I've been blessed with many people who have been willing to
share my sorrow, to just be sad with me. Others, however,
seem to want to rush me through my sadness. They want to
fix me. But I lost someone I loved dearly, and I'm sad.[40]

Jesus wept over the death of Lazarus and for his bereaved sisters,
Mary and Martha, not because he lost perspective but because he *had*
perspective. Death is an enemy, as is the suffering and disability that
precedes death. God hates it. So should we. We are to rejoice for the
coming day when God promises no more death and suffering. Such
rejoicing can fully coexist with mourning great loss.

We dare not wait for a time of crisis to learn how to worship God.
The Guthries worshiped God *in* crisis because they worshiped God
before the crisis. Trusting in God's sovereignty and goodness now will
sustain us when suffering comes later.

God, thank you for creating for us a destiny of eternal joy. Help us accept the fact that greater hardship now will mean greater joy forever. Thank you for using suffering to enlarge us as vessels to be filled with joy. The larger our capacity becomes, the greater the joy we will know. Help us to rejoice today for your goodness already shown to us and for the goodness you will never stop showing us in the ages to come.

54

Diamonds in the Darkness

The heavens proclaim the glory of God.
    The skies display his craftsmanship.
Day after day they continue to speak;
    night after night they make him known.
They speak without a sound or word;
    their voice is never heard.
Yet their message has gone throughout the earth,
    and their words to all the world.
God has made a home in the heavens for the sun.
It bursts forth like a radiant bridegroom after his wedding.
    It rejoices like a great athlete eager to run the race.

—PSALM 19:1–5, NLT

I fell in love with astronomy years before I fell in love with the Lord of the cosmos. Night after night I observed the marvels of planets, stars, nebulae, and galaxies. As every backyard astronomer knows, streetlights and bright moonlight obscure the wonders of the night sky.

In order to see the full glory of the stars, I learned that you must stay out for hours in the cold darkness. I did this night after night because what I discovered, and how it enriched my imagination, was worth it.

As the Heavens declare God's glory in the absence of other light, so God shows himself against the backdrop of evil and suffering—if only we are willing to look...and to discover that seeing him is worth even the cold darkness.

In the movie *Slumdog Millionaire,* the story's poverty, violence, crime, and child exploitation provide a backdrop for a young man's pure, unwavering love for a girl he met in the slums. The pair is tragically separated for years, and after they see each other briefly, she's taken from him again. Yet he never stops trying to find her.

Against impossible odds, the boy and girl finally reunite. He pulls back her *dupatta,* revealing a long, captor-inflicted scar that disfigures her face. As she looks down in shame, the young man, his eyes full of tears, holds up her face and kisses her scar. It's as if the scar itself is at last redeemed, somehow made beautiful.

That climactic, love-filled moment could not have happened without the story's disturbing setting of injustice, evil, suffering, and separation. He could not kiss her scar if she had no scar. Likewise, God could not wipe away all tears from every eye without the billions of tears shed because of the evil and suffering we've endured and inflicted (see Revelation 21:4).

If you put a diamond only in the light, you will see some of its wonders; but set it against something dark, *then* shine a light on it, and you will see magnificent beauty that otherwise would have remained invisible.

The gloomy backdrop of all human evil and suffering, including that of the cold, dark crucifixion itself, allows Jesus' grace and mercy to shine with dazzling brightness.

Thank you, Lord, for using the dark backdrop of my sin and the emptiness and alienation of my heart to forever enhance the brightness of your redeeming grace. I know I have been forgiven much; empower me now to love much. May I love with a love like yours and from yours: overflowing, spilling over onto those around me.

55

Trusting God's Plan

Praise be to the God and Father of our Lord Jesus Christ, who has blessed us in the heavenly realms with every spiritual blessing in Christ. For he chose us in him before the creation of the world to be holy and blameless in his sight. In love he predestined us to be adopted as his sons through Jesus Christ, in accordance with his pleasure and will—to the praise of his glorious grace, which he has freely given us in the One he loves. In him we have redemption through his blood, the forgiveness of sins, in accordance with the riches of God's grace that he lavished on us with all wisdom and understanding. And he made known to us the mystery of his will according to his good pleasure, which he purposed in Christ, to be put into effect when the times will have reached their fulfillment—to bring all things in heaven and on earth together under one head, even Christ.

—EPHESIANS 1:3–10

God chooses and predestines, he has a will and a wise plan, and nothing will thwart it. Instead of perplexing us, this should comfort us. Our lives, every aspect of them, have a purpose. The universe has a purpose, and it will be renewed and united together under the lordship of the King of kings. No evil being, no expression of free will, no random accident, no luck of the draw will prevent God from accomplishing his purpose.

In 1921, missionaries David and Svea Flood sensed God's leading to take the gospel to a remote area of the Belgian Congo called N'dolera.

Because a tribal chief would not let them enter his village, they had contact only with a young boy who sold them food. Svea led the boy to Jesus. Then malaria struck and within days of giving birth to a little girl, Svea died.

Stunned and disillusioned, David dug a crude grave, where he buried his young wife. David gave his baby girl, Aina, to another missionary couple—the Ericksons—and returned to Sweden embittered, saying God had ruined his life. Soon thereafter, the Ericksons died. Aina again had no one to care for her.

Why did this happen? What possible good could have come from it?

Stories like this have led countless people to conclude that even noble sacrifices can have pointless endings. But do they really?

American missionaries brought Aina to the United States, where she was adopted, becoming Aggie Hurst. Years later, a Swedish Christian magazine appeared in Aggie's mailbox. She didn't understand the words, but a photo inside shocked her—a grave with a white cross, marked with a name she recognized—that of her mother, Svea Flood.

A college professor translated the article for Aggie: Missionaries came to N'dolera long ago… A white baby was born… The young mother died… One little African boy was led to Christ… The boy grew up and built a school in the village. Gradually he won his students to Christ… The children led their parents to Christ… Even the tribal chief became a Christian.

After decades of bitterness, one day an old and ill David Flood had a visitor—his daughter, Aina Flood, now Aggie Hurst. She told David the story recounted in the article. She informed her father, "Today there are six hundred African people serving Christ because you and mother were faithful to God's call in your life."

David was stunned. His heart softened. He returned to God. Weeks later, he died.

Aggie eventually met that African boy, by then superintendent of a national church in Zaire (formerly the Belgian Congo, now the Democratic Republic of the Congo), an association of 110,000 baptized believers.[41]

The great tragedy in the lives of David, Svea, and Aina Flood was undeniably heartbreaking. It appeared utterly cruel and pointless. But in time it yielded a great harvest of joy that will continue for eternity.

Lord, the first chapter of Ephesians tells us not only that you chose and predestined us and that you have a purpose

for us, but that you have lavished upon us your grace. You have done so in all wisdom so that your plan is seldom obvious but requires us to trust you. Help us to put no false gods before you, including the idols of money, sex, power, fame, and self-sufficiency. Remind us that you alone are worthy of our trust, that you alone can bear the weight of it.

56

Grace: A Light in Dark Times

Therefore, since we have been justified through faith, we have peace with God through our Lord Jesus Christ, through whom we have gained access by faith into this grace in which we now stand. And we rejoice in the hope of the glory of God. Not only so, but we also rejoice in our sufferings, because we know that suffering produces perseverance; perseverance, character; and character, hope. And hope does not disappoint us, because God has poured out his love into our hearts by the Holy Spirit, whom he has given us.

—ROMANS 5:1–5

God tells us that suffering isn't pointless. We are to rejoice in our sufferings because of the outcomes they will produce: perseverance, character, hope, and the certain expectation that God will make all things right and work all things for our good and his glory.

Some of the most meaningful victories in our lives come in the context of our most difficult, seemingly useless suffering.

Howard Hendricks tells of visiting a leprosy center in India. The morning he arrived, the residents were gathered for a praise service. One of the women with leprosy hobbled to the platform. Hendricks said that even though she was partially blind and badly disfigured, she was one of the most beautiful women he'd ever seen.

Raising both of her nearly fingerless hands toward Heaven, she said in a clear voice, "I want to praise God that I am a leper because it was through my leprosy that I came to know Jesus Christ as my Savior. And I would rather be a leper who knows Christ than be completely whole and a stranger to His grace."[42]

Seeing God's hand in our adversities comes in many different forms.

After serving in a ministry for fifteen years, Dan endured a ten-year spiritual drought. He told me, "I felt like God just wasn't there. My spiritual life became pointless."

Finally, Dan determined to draw near to God, hoping God would keep his promise to draw near to him (see James 4:8). Ten Saturdays in a row he took a chair into the woods and sat for hours at a time. He vowed he would keep coming until "God showed up." He brought pen and paper to write reflections. For the first nine weeks he sensed no contact with God and so had little to write.

On the tenth Saturday, suddenly Dan started writing. He felt God's presence like a gentle wave, for the first time in ten years. Beginning that day, his life changed. He told me, "As miserable as those years were, I would not trade it for anything, because God showed me that my earlier fifteen years of Christian life and ministry had really been about me, not him. I had lived on my terms, not his. At last I was seeing God."

Dan said, "After it was all over, I thanked God for those ten years." Yet during that dark time, Dan said he couldn't have imagined *ever* being grateful for it.

Since detailed past, present, and future knowledge is unavailable to us, we sometimes see negative circumstances as random and pointless. We do not see that God has and will accomplish good purposes through them. Who but God is wise enough to know...or powerful enough to make it happen?

Lord, your Word promises that we will forever benefit from character building that makes us more Christlike. You also reveal to us that suffering is a primary instrument you use to bring this about. While it seems counterintuitive to rejoice in our sufferings, you tell us to do so. Give us the ability to trust that what you've told us is true and that you know best, thereby revealing the light of joy in the midst of our darkness.

57

Promises Kept

You, however, know all about my teaching, my way of life, my purpose, faith, patience, love, endurance, persecutions, sufferings—what kinds of things happened to me in Antioch, Iconium and Lystra, the persecutions I endured. Yet the Lord rescued me from all of them. In fact, everyone who wants to live a godly life in Christ Jesus will be persecuted, while evil men and impostors will go from bad to worse, deceiving and being deceived. But as for you, continue in what you have learned and have become convinced of, because you know those from whom you learned it, and how from infancy you have known the holy Scriptures, which are able to make you wise for salvation through faith in Christ Jesus. All Scripture is God-breathed and is useful for teaching, rebuking, correcting and training in righteousness, so that the man of God may be thoroughly equipped for every good work.

—2 TIMOTHY 3:10–17

veryone who wants to live a Christ-centered life will be persecuted. And *everyone* really does mean everyone, which is why all the Greek scholars translate this passage that way.

God promises us suffering. It's not a promise we're quick to claim, it's not one of our favorite memory verses, but there it is, just as inspired and true as John 3:16 or whatever our life verse might be.

Even at its best, the ancient world offered a hard life. Christians *routinely* suffered. They still do. Even Christians who don't suffer persecution still pull weeds, experience pain in childbirth, and become ill and die, just like everyone else.

The health and wealth gospel's claims are so obviously opposed to countless biblical passages that it is difficult to imagine, apart from the deceptive powers of Satan, how so many Christians could actually believe them. We overrate health and underrate holiness. If physical health is our primary value, then why endanger it for a higher cause? While earlier Christians risked their lives to serve those dying from the bubonic plague, prosperity theology tends to encourage believers to flee from threatening ministry opportunities so that they might cling to what they cannot preserve anyway.

Emmanuel Ndikumana explained why he returned home to Burundi even though the Hutu-Tutsi conflict there threatened his life. Out of revenge for atrocities, Tutsis had already killed his Hutu father and grandfather. Emmanuel told me, "I do not condemn those who fled; I understand. But I felt I should not treasure safety. The only way for me to prove to my people that I believed the gospel was to return and suffer with them. If I fear death as unbelievers do, I have nothing to offer unbelievers. Only when you are free from the fear of death are you really free."

A woman who had based her life on the health and wealth world-view lay dying of cancer. She looked into a camera during an interview and said, "I've lost my faith." She felt bitter that God had "broken his promises." She correctly realized that the god she'd followed does not exist. She incorrectly concluded that the God of the Bible had let her down. He hadn't; her church and its preachers had done that. God had never made the promises that she thought he'd broken.

When hard times come, people should lose their faith in false doctrine, not in God. In contrast to jewelry-flaunting televangelists, Paul said, "We must go through many hardships to enter the kingdom of God" (Acts 14:22). If you are a Christian, God will deliver you from *eternal* suffering. And even now he will give you joyful foretastes of living in his presence. *That's* his promise.

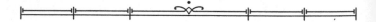

Father, keep us from being pulled into the black hole of prosperity theology. Help us see it for the false gospel it is. You promise us hardship, and you deliver on your promise. But suffering isn't just something to endure; it's something we can trust you to use for your purposes, to strengthen us and transform our hearts and expand the platform for our ministry to others. Help us not to follow false prophets of health and wealth but rather the humble example of those like Emmanuel Ndikumana, who learned in suffering that it is disobedience we should fear, not death.

58

Exchanging Temporary for Eternal

Dear friends, do not be surprised at the painful trial you are suffering, as though something strange were happening to you. But rejoice that you participate in the sufferings of Christ, so that you may be overjoyed when his glory is revealed. If you are insulted because of the name of Christ, you are blessed, for the Spirit of glory and of God rests on you. If you suffer, it should not be as a murderer or thief or any other kind of criminal, or even as a meddler. However, if you suffer as a Christian, do not be ashamed, but praise God that you bear that name. For it is time for judgment to begin with the family of God; and if it begins with us, what will the outcome be for those who do not obey the gospel of God? And,

"If it is hard for the righteous to be saved,

what will become of the ungodly and the sinner?"

So then, those who suffer according to God's will should commit themselves to their faithful Creator and continue to do good.

—1 PETER 4:12–19

I have to smile whenever I read this passage. God tells us we shouldn't be surprised when we suffer "as though something strange were happening to you." It's like he's saying, "Whatever gave you the idea that you weren't supposed to suffer?"

While researching prosperity theology, I've read many books that emphatically say it is not God's will for his children to suffer. Yet the inspired Word of God says "those who suffer according to God's will should commit themselves to their faithful Creator and continue to do good." Who are you going to believe? God gets my vote.

If your goal is to avoid suffering in this life, then following Christ will not help you. Jesus himself said, "If the world hates you, keep in mind that it hated me first…. If they persecuted me, they will persecute you also" (John 15:18, 20).

Decades ago, Josef Tson was the best-known pastor in Romania. At a time when the Christian faith had become virtually illegal, he openly preached the gospel, and believers circulated his recordings throughout Romania. Police threatened him repeatedly with imprisonment and arrest. In his sixties he studied at Oxford for his doctorate, writing a dissertation that became a book titled *Suffering, Martyrdom, and Rewards in Heaven*.

I first opened the Scriptures with Josef in 1988 with a group of theologians discussing eternal rewards. Twenty years later, when writing my book *If God Is Good*, I remembered his stories and insights and called him. Josef explained to me how the belief that God doesn't want his people to suffer once corrupted the Romanian church. In the interests of self-preservation, he said, they failed to speak out against injustice, tyranny, and the idolatry of turning men into gods. He recalls joining the crowd on the streets and crying, "Glory to Stalin."

God convicted Josef. As a pastor he then refused to glorify communist leaders and started to speak out boldly for Christ. Interrogators threatened him with death every day for six months. Finally he told them, "Your supreme weapon is killing. My supreme weapon is dying. My preaching will speak ten times louder after you kill me."

Finally, in 1981, the Romanian government exiled him.

In health and wealth circles, leadership credibility is measured by jets, jewelry, and invitations to the White House. In contrast to the prosperity preachers of his day, whom he mockingly called "super-apostles," Paul argued for his own credibility as God's servant based on his "troubles, hardships and distresses; in beatings, imprisonments and riots; in hard work, sleepless nights and hunger" (2 Corinthians 6:4–5).

I don't like suffering. Nor am I called to seek it. But when we bend over backward to avoid it and value comfort over commitment, we are not acting as Christ's disciples. It's not our job to be safe or popular. We exist solely to please an Audience of One.

Father, thank you for the examples you've given us, not only in the Bible but throughout church history. Help us look to people like the reformers and pioneer missionaries and ordinary people who have suffered for the gospel, for they draw our eyes to you. Prompt us to turn off the television and read their stories instead of following the idols of popular culture. Help us turn our eyes away from glory-hungry prosperity preachers who spread a mammon-infested gospel that is truer in America than in Haiti and therefore not true.

59

Permanent Healing

There is a time for everything,
    and a season for every activity under heaven:
    a time to be born and a time to die,
    a time to plant and a time to uproot,
    a time to kill and a time to heal,
    a time to tear down and a time to build,
    a time to weep and a time to laugh,
    a time to mourn and a time to dance,
    a time to scatter stones and a time to gather them,
    a time to embrace and a time to refrain,
    a time to search and a time to give up,
    a time to keep and a time to throw away,
    a time to tear and a time to mend,
    a time to be silent and a time to speak,
    a time to love and a time to hate,
    a time for war and a time for peace.

—ECCLESIASTES 3:1–8

There is indeed a time to be born and a time to die, a time to weep and a time to laugh. There is also a promised time that awaits God's children, when life will swallow up death and laughter will eclipse our tears.

Julia was a powerful woman who flaunted her beauty and wealth. Her volatile temper and sharp tongue put people in their place and left a trail of damaged relationships.

Then, in her midforties, Julia was diagnosed with an aggressive cancer. Despite treatment, the disease progressed. Doctors said she had less than a year to live.

Julia's diagnosis frightened her; she sought spiritual counsel, started reading the New Testament, confessed her sins, and gave her life to Jesus Christ. She wrote letters, made phone calls, invited people for coffee, and sought forgiveness from the many she'd hurt. She did all she could to restore relationships with family and others. She made peace with her ex-husband, grew close to her children, and developed a loving circle of Christian friends.

Several weeks before she died, Julia told her pastor that she considered her cancer to be a love gift from God. Julia said she would gladly exchange all her years of beauty, wealth, and influence for the two years of illness that taught her the unspeakable joy of loving Jesus and loving others.[43]

In contrast to Julia, however, many people—after a terminal diagnosis—spend the remainder of their lives searching for a scientific cure or a spiritual healing or both. I don't, of course, fault sick people for seeking a cure! But, like Julia, we should focus our energies not simply on *avoiding* death but on investing our time in *preparing* for it—getting right with God and ministering to others.

While resisting death and fighting for life can be virtuous, it can also degenerate into idolatry if staying alive here becomes more important than everything else. I have several friends diagnosed with terminal illnesses, and I am praying boldly for their healing. But should God heal them completely, they will still ultimately die, as will we all unless Christ comes within our lifetime. Have you noticed there are no 120-year-old faith healers? Paul had it right: "Christ will be exalted in my body, whether by life or by death. For to me, to live is Christ and to die is gain" (Philippians 1:20–21).

If God has healed you, rejoice! God can and does heal, and we should celebrate his mercy. But all healing in this world is temporary. Resurrection healing will be permanent. For that, our hearts should overflow with praise to our gracious God.

Father, thank you for being the Great Physician, the Healer of hearts and minds and bodies. Help us understand both the reality that there is a time for life to begin in this world and a time for life to end and that you are sovereign over both. Embolden us to pray for healing but always to pray for your glory and the eternal good of those who are suffering. Make us eternity-minded rather than shortsighted. Give us strength to cling to the promise of the day when you will, in the resurrection, fulfill your Calvary-bought promise of complete and eternal healing.

60

Perfected by Suffering

"What is man that you are mindful of him,
    the son of man that you care for him?
You made him a little lower than the angels;
    you crowned him with glory and honor
    and put everything under his feet."
In putting everything under him, God left nothing that is not
subject to him. Yet at present we do not see everything subject
to him. But we see Jesus, who was made a little lower than the
angels, now crowned with glory and honor because he suffered
death, so that by the grace of God he might taste death for
everyone.

In bringing many sons to glory, it was fitting that God,
for whom and through whom everything exists, should make
the author of their salvation perfect through suffering. Both
the one who makes men holy and those who are made holy
are of the same family. So Jesus is not ashamed to call them
brothers.

—Hebrews 2:6–11

J esus was morally perfect from his conception, but Scripture tells us he grew in knowledge and understanding through his life experiences. In that sense he became more perfect, that is more complete, through his suffering. Now, if the Father used suffering to bring Jesus to maturity, surely he can use it to do that for us.

Have you ever heard anyone say, "I grew closest to God when my life was free from pain and suffering"? No, it's the opposite. God uses adversity and suffering to help us grow and mature.

Josef Tson, who faced much evil in communist Romania, told me, "This world, with all its evil, is God's deliberately chosen environment for people to grow in their characters. The character and trustworthiness we form here, we take with us there, to Heaven. Romans and 1 Peter make clear that suffering is a grace from God. It is a grace given us now to prepare us for living forever."

Mountain climbers could save time and energy if they reached the summit in a helicopter, but their ultimate purpose is conquest, not efficiency. Sure, they want to reach a goal, but they want to do so the hard way, by testing their character and resolve.

God could create scientists, mathematicians, athletes, and musicians. He doesn't. He creates children who take on those roles over a long process. We learn to excel by handling failure. Only in cultivating discipline, endurance, and patience do we find satisfaction and reward.

If cancer or paralysis or a car accident prompts us to draw on God's strength to become more conformed to Christ, then regardless of the human, demonic, or natural forces involved, God will be glorified in it. My writer friend, Stephanie Grace Whitson, wrote this to me after her husband Bob's death:

One thing that I've become convinced of is that God has different definitions for words than I do. For example, He does work all things for my eternal good and His eternal glory. But his definition of *good* is different than mine. My "good" would never include cancer and young widowhood. My "good" would include healing and dying together in our sleep when we are in our nineties. But cancer was good because of what God did that He couldn't do any other way. Cancer was, in fact, necessary to make Bob and me look more like Jesus. So in love, God allowed what was best for us...in light of eternity.

Lord Jesus, in the merger of your deity and humanity, you chose not to tap into the fullness of your divine attributes so that you actually learned and grew in wisdom and maturity. We don't pretend to understand this. We know that you suffered for us on Earth, tasting death for everyone, and as a result you are now crowned with glory and honor. And though we deserve only Hell, you have not only redeemed us but also have told us that as we faithfully serve you now, we will one day participate in the reward of glory and honor with you. As an athlete might wish that he could excel without the rigors of training, we could wish that the path to that eternal reward did not involve suffering. But it does. Thanks for showing us that it's worth it. As we face our own suffering, help us to trust you for that now.

61

Put to Good Use

In a large house there are articles not only of gold and silver, but also of wood and clay; some are for noble purposes and some for ignoble. If a man cleanses himself from the latter, he will be an instrument for noble purposes, made holy, useful to the Master and prepared to do any good work.

—2 TIMOTHY 2:20–21

We all end up being instruments for some purpose. The question is whether we will be instruments for God's great and noble purposes or for some lesser or even dishonorable purposes.

When Christ's disciples asked whose sin accounted for a man born blind, Jesus said, "Neither this man nor his parents sinned" (John 9:3). Jesus then redirected his disciples from thinking about the *cause* of the man's disability to considering the *purpose* for it. He said, "This happened *so that* the work of God might be displayed in his life." Eugene Peterson paraphrases Christ's words this way: "You're asking the wrong question. You're looking for someone to blame. There is no such cause-effect here. Look instead for what God can do" (MSG).

Nick Vujicic entered this world without arms or legs. His parents, both committed Christians, felt devastated by their firstborn son's condition. "If God is a God of love," they said, "then why would he let something like this happen?" But they chose to trust God despite their questions.

Nick struggled at school, where other students bullied and rejected him. Meanwhile, he recalls, "I still got hung up on the fact that if God really loved me, why did He make me like this? I wondered if I'd done something wrong and began to feel certain that this must be true."

Thoughts of suicide plagued Nick until one day the fifteen-year-old read the story in John 9 about the man born blind: "that the works of God should be revealed in him" (NKJV). He surrendered his life to Christ. Now, in his midtwenties, he's earned a bachelor's degree and encourages others as a motivational speaker.

Nick says:

> God began to instill a passion for sharing my story and experiences to help others cope with whatever challenge they might have in their lives. Turning my struggles into something that would glorify God and bless others, I realized my purpose! The Lord was going to use me to encourage and inspire others to live to their fullest potential and not let anything get in the way of accomplishing their hopes and dreams. God's purpose became clearer to me, and now I'm fully convinced and understand that His glory is revealed as He uses me just the way I am. And even more wonderful, He can use me in ways others can't be used.[44]

Lord, I don't know what purposes Nick Vujicic would be serving now if not for his disability, but I suspect they would be less great and less noble. I know that my life hardships, which have been far smaller, have been used by you to make me a more functional vessel for your kingdom work. Had you withheld from me those adversities, I think I would be more self-absorbed and self-assured, less grateful and aware of my profound need to depend on your sovereign grace. Thank you for having the wisdom to choose for me what I would never have chosen for myself. Make us cleansed and constructive instruments today, Lord, for your glory and our good.

62

A Masterpiece Under God's Chisel

For it is by grace you have been saved, through faith—and this not from yourselves, it is the gift of God—not by works, so that no one can boast. For we are God's workmanship, created in Christ Jesus to do good works, which God prepared in advance for us to do.

—EPHESIANS 2:8–10

God is a master craftsman, an artist with incomparable skill. He created humanity in his image, but his creation became seriously damaged in the Fall. Through his redemptive work, God recreated us in Christ, empowering us to do a lifetime of good works to his glory. But even with our reclamation, we have many imperfections in need of the Master's refinement.

When Nanci and I saw *David* in Florence, it (my instinct is to say *he*) took our breath away. To produce his masterpiece, Michelangelo chose a stone that all other artists had rejected. Seeing that huge marble block's hidden potential, he chipped away everything that wasn't David. The master worked daily to transform it into something surpassingly beautiful.

Now, if marble had feelings, it wouldn't like the chiseling process. It might resent the sculptor.

While Michelangelo may not have called upon the stone to cooperate with him, God has called us to yield ourselves by submitting to his chisel. Because we fail to see the person God intends to form through our adversity, we too may resent the chiseling. The Master Artist chose us, the flawed and unusable, to be crafted into the image of Christ to fulfill our destiny in displaying Jesus to the watching universe.

We ask God to remove the chisel because it hurts, but it's a means of transformation: "And we, who with unveiled faces all reflect the Lord's glory, are being transformed into his likeness with ever-increasing glory" (2 Corinthians 3:18).

God doesn't simply want us to *feel* good. He wants us to *be* good. And very often, the road to being good involves pain.

Joni Eareckson Tada writes, "Before my paralysis, my hands reached for a lot of wrong things, and my feet took me into some bad places. After my paralysis, tempting choices were scaled down considerably. My particular affliction is divinely hand-tailored expressly for me. Nobody has to suffer 'transverse spinal lesion at the fourth-fifth cervical' exactly as I did to be conformed to his image."[45]

God uses suffering to purge sin from our lives, strengthen our commitment to him, force us to depend on his grace, bind us together with other believers, yield discernment, foster sensitivity, discipline our minds, impart wisdom, stretch our hope, cause us to know Christ better, make us long for truth, lead us to repentance of sin, teach us to give thanks in times of sorrow, increase our faith, and strengthen our character. And once he accomplishes such great things, often we can see in part what we will one day see in full—that our suffering has been worth it.

Lord, though you have redeemed us, we are yet incomplete, in need of your daily touch and refinement. Thank you for using adverse circumstances, disappointment, discouragement, frustration, and uncertainty, along with our ailments, to transform us into Christ's likeness. May we submit ourselves to your chisel, making transformation easier for us and more honoring to you.

63

Proof of God's Eternal Goodness

I will praise you, O Lord my God, with all my heart;
 I will glorify your name forever.
For great is your love toward me;
 you have delivered me from the depths of the grave.
The arrogant are attacking me, O God;
 a band of ruthless men seeks my life—
 men without regard for you.
But you, O Lord, are a compassionate and gracious God,
 slow to anger, abounding in love and faithfulness.
Turn to me and have mercy on me;
 grant your strength to your servant
 and save the son of your maidservant.
Give me a sign of your goodness,
 that my enemies may see it and be put to shame,
 for you, O LORD, have helped me and comforted me.

—PSALM 86:12–17

Affirming by faith God's compassion, grace, faithfulness, and love, his child—wanting to see clearer evidence—cries out to God, "Give me a sign of your goodness."

When someone survives an accident or receives a negative biopsy report, we sigh in relief and say, "God is good." We're right to give heartfelt thanks. But God remains just as good if the person dies or the biopsy report brings bad news. *God is good even when we can't see it.*

My friend, writer Ethel Herr, had a double mastectomy, then discovered two months later that the cancer had spread. She told our group of writers:

> God has been preparing me for this moment. He has under-
> girded me in ways I've never known before. He has made
> Himself increasingly real and precious to me. He has given to
> me JOY such as I've never known before—and I've no need to
> work at it, it just comes, even amidst the tears. He has taught
> me that no matter how good my genes are or how well I take
> care of my diet and myself, He will lead me on whatever
> journey He chooses and will never leave me for a moment of
> that journey. And He planned it all in such a way that step by
> step, He prepared me for the moment when the doctor
> dropped the last shoe.... God is good, no matter what the
> diagnosis or the prognosis, or the fearfulness of the uncer-
> tainty of having neither. The key to knowing God is good is
> simply knowing Him.[46]

Sometimes God intervenes by removing our suffering. Often he comforts us in our suffering. Sometimes he holds our hands as he brings us home to the perfect world he's made for us. May he give us eyes to see how he demonstrates that love every day in hundreds of ways, most of which we take for granted. In our suffering, God shows us his goodness, grace, and compassion.

We won't all, in this life, meet someone whose story will suddenly shed light on God's purpose in *our* loved one's suffering or death. But I think most of us will have that very experience one day, beyond the ends of this Earth, on that New Earth, where we, eyes wide, will hear countless jaw-dropping stories of God's sovereign grace.

How true it is, Lord, that you are good…all the time. Grant us the perspective to see this truth regardless of our circumstances, as you have granted my friend Ethel. As the psalmist prayed, we ask for your mercy, strength, patience, love, and faithfulness. And this very day, Lord, would you give us each a sign of your goodness? Either that, or give us eyes to see the countless signs you have already posted around us every day of our lives.

64

A Firm Foundation for New Life

But the gift is not like the trespass. For if the many died by the trespass of the one man, how much more did God's grace and the gift that came by the grace of the one man, Jesus Christ, overflow to the many! Again, the gift of God is not like the result of the one man's sin: The judgment followed one sin and brought condemnation, but the gift followed many trespasses and brought justification. For if, by the trespass of the one man, death reigned through that one man, how much more will those who receive God's abundant provision of grace and of the gift of righteousness reign in life through the one man, Jesus Christ.

Consequently, just as the result of one trespass was condemnation for all men, so also the result of one act of righteousness was justification that brings life for all men. For just as through the disobedience of the one man the many were made sinners, so also through the obedience of the one man the many will be made righteous.

—ROMANS 5:15–19

The grace of Jesus isn't an add-on or makeover that enhances our lives. It causes a radical transformation of our lives. Religions can alter behavior. Only Jesus has the power to transform the heart. Only the work of Jesus is the foundation on which we can build a new life.

Action International, www.actionintl.org, works with street children in the Philippines. One of them is Wendy. Her father died and her mom's boyfriend abused her, so Wendy ran away. She soon found herself forced into servitude. She ran away again and met a Christian woman who took her into her family. She attended Bible studies and a camp for street kids, where she gave her life to Christ. She was mentored, began teaching a children's Bible class, and soon will graduate from Bible college.

Lino was a drug addict who slept on sidewalks. At an Action International camp for street kids, he chose to follow Christ. The local church trained him in the Scriptures, hired him as a janitor, and then sponsored Lino through a five-year pastoral course. Now he serves as a pastor, Bible teacher, and counselor.

Enrico suffered abuse as a houseboy. Later, as a drug addict, he joined a gang heavily involved in crime and witchcraft. One day he went out to recruit for the gang. Instead, a Christian recruited him to attend a camp for street kids. Eventually his heart softened, and Enrico trusted Christ. His life changed dramatically. Lino and others trained him in the Scriptures, gave him work, and helped him graduate from high school. Enrico now works on a farm as a true follower of Jesus Christ.

Society had cast off Wendy, Lino, and Enrico as unloved and abused street kids, hopeless victims—and probable future perpetrators—of evil and suffering. Finding themselves at the bottom, their hearts opened to God's offer of rescue. Had they grown up in whole families, with lots of money and security, they might never have met those Christians who modeled for them the love of Jesus.

Sometimes God delivers us from suffering, and other times he sustains us through suffering. Sometimes God calms the storm, and sometimes he calms the heart. Both are acts of grace, and both should prompt us to praise him.

Lord, you are the justifier of sinners and the transformer of the ungodly. Help us never to underestimate your power to change anyone's heart, including our own. The incomparable gift of your grace has accomplished the ultimate miracle—it has made us righteous. And no evil inflicted upon us, no suffering we endure, can take away your miracle of grace. On the contrary, they will give you only greater opportunity to extend your life-changing power in us.

65

God's Grace Is Sufficient

To keep me from becoming conceited because of these surpassingly great revelations, there was given me a thorn in my flesh, a messenger of Satan, to torment me. Three times I pleaded with the Lord to take it away from me. But he said to me, "My grace is sufficient for you, for my power is made perfect in weakness." Therefore I will boast all the more gladly about my weaknesses, so that Christ's power may rest on me. That is why, for Christ's sake, I delight in weaknesses, in insults, in hardships, in persecutions, in difficulties. For when I am weak, then I am strong.

—2 CORINTHIANS 12:7–10

The apostle Paul didn't deny the extent of his suffering. Rather, he identified the thorn in his flesh—some kind of disability or disease—as a source of real torment. He further recognized that it had been sent to him by Satan, who no doubt wanted to derail him from loving Christ and serving him.

But due to God's sufficient grace and Paul's surrender to God's power and purposes, Paul could say he actually delighted in insults, hardship, persecution, and difficulties. This isn't denial or masochism or attempting to sound spiritual. It is recognizing that in the weakness of our suffering, God must empower us. And God will get the glory for doing so.

Suffering in a life spent pleasing God often looks indistinguishable from suffering persecution. Paul juxtaposed sickness and sleepless nights with beatings and scourgings. He linked shipwreck and shivering to being stoned for the gospel (see 2 Corinthians 11:23–28).

The point is not the degree of evil intended against us but our faithfulness in suffering. So regardless of why we suffer, God can use it to deepen our faith: "Rejoice that you participate in the sufferings of Christ, so that you may be overjoyed when his glory is revealed.… Those who suffer according to God's will should commit themselves to their faithful Creator and continue to do good" (1 Peter 4:13, 19).

David Guthrie, reflecting on the death of his disabled daughter, told me, "I spent my life waiting for the other shoe to drop. The shoe has dropped. I had thought I was invulnerable. Now I know better. I thought, *Our child has died. How much worse can it get?* There's less to fear. God will be enough for us. Now we say it out of experience."

Instead of blaming doctors, drunk drivers, and criminals for our suffering, we should look for what God can accomplish through it.

Fanny Crosby, blinded by an incompetent doctor at the age of six weeks, penned more than eight thousand hymns. She expressed delight that Jesus' face would be the first she would ever see. If she'd thought, "I'll never be able to see," she would have been profoundly sad. Instead, she could say with Job, "After my skin has been destroyed, yet in my flesh I will see God;… I, and not another" (Job 19:26–27).

Concerning her blindness, Fanny said, "It seemed intended by the blessed providence of God that I should be blind all my life, and I thank him for the dispensation.… If perfect earthly sight were offered me tomorrow I would not accept it.… I verily believe it was His intention that I should live my days in physical darkness, so as to be better prepared to sing His praises and incite others so to do."[47]

Sometimes we may resent God for imposing unwanted difficulties on us. If we see through the lens of eternity, however, that resentment changes to thanksgiving for God's grace and power. We praise him for being glorified in our weakness and for making us better and ultimately happier people, even if it costs us temporary pain and extreme inconvenience.

Like the apostle Paul and Fanny Crosby and countless others, Lord, help us today to look at our thorns in the flesh, our weaknesses and ailments, and consider how you use them as opportunities to reveal your grace and strength. Counterintuitive as it may seem, help us delight in our weakness and in the knowledge that you can be glorified through giving us supernatural empowerment, grace, and perspective and by touching others through us as a result.

66

Trading Shallow for Deep

Have mercy on me, O God, have mercy on me,
    for in you my soul takes refuge.
I will take refuge in the shadow of your wings
    until the disaster has passed.
I cry out to God Most High,
    to God, who fulfills his purpose for me.…
Be exalted, O God, above the heavens;
    let your glory be over all the earth.…
My heart is steadfast, O God,
    my heart is steadfast;
    I will sing and make music.
Awake, my soul!
    Awake, harp and lyre!
    I will awaken the dawn.
I will praise you, O Lord, among the nations;
    I will sing of you among the peoples.
For great is your love, reaching to the heavens;
    your faithfulness reaches to the skies.
Be exalted, O God, above the heavens;
    let your glory be over all the earth.

—Psalm 57:1–2, 5, 7–11

My wife, Nanci, suffered through what she calls her "year of fear and free-floating anxiety that made me fall in love with God." Nanci has known God from childhood and trusted him all through my arrests, lawsuits, and job loss, then through her mother's death and other losses (and threatened ones). But that inexplicable year of her life, unrelated to any outside traumatic event, changed her. She coped by telling God, morning and night, how much she loved him.

She has continued her habit of praise and intimacy with God that developed when daily fear and dread fell upon her. The crushing emotions of that time have departed; the sense of intimacy with her Savior remains. To this day, Nanci rejoices in God's love for her and her love for him in ways she never would have known without that year she otherwise could describe as hellish.

In the midst of our suffering, God makes some of his most profound and precious self-revelations. Perhaps he does so because only then are we ready to hear them.

Josef Tson writes, "During the time I was expecting to be crushed by the Romanian secret police interrogators, God became more real to me than ever before or after in my life. It is difficult to put into words the experience I had with God at that time. It was like a rapture into a sweet and total communion with the Beloved. God's test for me then became the pathway to a special knowledge of the reality of God."

Josef continued, "God achieves great things in the world through the one who accepts His way of suffering and self-sacrifice. In the end, however, it turns out that the greatest things are achieved in the sufferer himself. The one who sacrificially accepts to be a blessing for others discovers that, in the final analysis, he is the one who has harvested the greatest blessings."[48]

"Without Christ not one step," David Livingstone declared, "with Him anywhere."[49]

Suffering can help us know God and prepare us to trade a shallow life not worth keeping for a deeper life we'll never lose.

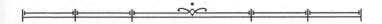

Father, I join my beloved Nanci in thanking you for that very difficult year in her life. You used it to draw her closer to you, just as you have used other painful times for our good and your glory. You know best, and we entrust ourselves to you. Help us to take no step without you.

67

In Everything, Give Thanks

To the roots of the mountains I sank down;
 the earth beneath barred me in forever.
But you brought my life up from the pit,
 O LORD my God.
When my life was ebbing away,
 I remembered you, LORD,
and my prayer rose to you,
 to your holy temple.
Those who cling to worthless idols
 forfeit the grace that could be theirs.
But I, with a song of thanksgiving,
 will sacrifice to you.
What I have vowed I will make good.
 Salvation comes from the LORD.

—JONAH 2:6–9

Jonah praised God who rescued him from the pit—in his case the belly of a great fish, an exceedingly unpleasant place. Just thinking about it makes me grateful that no matter what else happens to me today, it won't likely include sloshing around in the digestive system of a giant sea creature. Already I feel better about the rest of this day!

Reflecting on God's rescue from the plight he'd brought upon himself through disobedience, Jonah is thankful and becomes motivated to make personal sacrifices to serve God more faithfully.

Elisabeth Elliot, one of my heroes, writes, "On one of those terrible days during my husband's cancer, when he could hardly bear the pain or the thought of yet another treatment, and I could hardly bear to bear it with him, we remarked on how wonderful it would be to have just a single ordinary day."[50]

How many of us fail to express gratitude for those ordinary days, wishing instead for something better? If you've had a single ordinary day recently, why not thank God for it? Don't wait for an extraordinary day when you feel wonderful and everything goes your way. That day may not come. And if it does, God's hand will be no more in it than in all your other days.

Puritan pastor Richard Baxter wrote, "Resolve to spend most of your time in thanksgiving and praising God. If you cannot do it with the joy that you should, yet do it as you can.… Doing it as you can is the way to be able to do it better. Thanksgiving stirreth up thankfulness in the heart."[51]

Baxter is right—expressing gratitude makes a grateful heart. Children who learn to say thanks become more thankful. Gratitude is a perspective-shaping habit.

Gratitude never comes from avoiding difficulty but from finding yourself sustained through it. The degree of joy rises to the degree of gratitude, and the level of gratitude corresponds to the level of God's grace experienced in our suffering. God's sustaining providence brings relief, even when life becomes unspeakably difficult.

Corrie ten Boom's sister Betsie, in light of the command, "Give thanks in all circumstances" (1 Thessalonians 5:18), insisted they should thank God even for the fleas and lice in their concentration camp barracks. Corrie resisted until she realized that the fleas and lice made it possible for her to open the Bible and teach it unhindered to other prisoners. Guards could have confiscated her forbidden Bible, but they refused to enter because of the vermin.[52] Think of it—God even works through parasites, though rarely can we see his work as clearly as Corrie finally did.

Cultivating thankfulness today will allow us to cling to God's goodness and mercy in our darkest hours. Those hours may yet lie ahead of us—but beyond them stretch unending millennia of inexpressible joy that we will appreciate more deeply because of these fleeting days of darkness.

Father, as you rescued Jonah from the great fish, you will rescue us from lesser calamities, and in some cases perhaps greater ones. Help us to be grateful for ordinary days. And during our bad days, remind us of what you are preparing for us—endless days filled with goodness and abundance, where we will look back with amazed delight at your deliverance and look forward with anticipation of the endless wonders yet to come.

68

Blessed by Affliction

To the arrogant I say, "Boast no more,"
    and to the wicked, "Do not lift up your horns.
Do not lift your horns against heaven;
    do not speak with outstretched neck."
No one from the east or the west
    or from the desert can exalt a man.
But it is God who judges:
    He brings one down, he exalts another.
In the hand of the LORD is a cup
    full of foaming wine mixed with spices;
he pours it out, and all the wicked of the earth
    drink it down to its very dregs.
As for me, I will declare this forever;
    I will sing praise to the God of Jacob.

—PSALM 75:4–9

God is the Almighty Judge who brings one person down
while exalting another with purposes and timing that only

he understands. His creatures may respond to his mysterious ways with bitterness, indifference, or praise. Given these alternatives, I choose praise.

Charles Spurgeon wrote, "I venture to say that the greatest earthly blessing that God can give to any of us is health, with the possible exception of sickness.... If some men that I know of could only be favoured with a month of rheumatism, it would, by God's grace, mellow them marvelously."[53]

Though he sought to avoid suffering, Spurgeon said, "I am afraid that all the grace that I have got of my comfortable and easy times and happy hours, might almost lie on a penny. But the good that I have received from my sorrows, and pains, and griefs, is altogether incalculable.... Affliction is the best bit of furniture in my house. It is the best book in a minister's library."[54]

You may think, *I refuse to accept that suffering can prove worthwhile.* But your rejection of God's goodness will not make you better or happier; it will only bring resentment and greater pain. Accept health as God's blessing and its absence as God's severe mercy. Samuel Rutherford wrote these profound words in the seventeenth century:

> If God had told me some time ago that he was about to make me as happy as I could be in this world, and then had told me that he should begin by crippling me in arm or limb, and removing me from all my usual sources of enjoyment, I should have thought it a very strange mode of accomplishing his purpose. And yet, how is his wisdom manifest even in this! For if you should see a man shut up in a closed room, idolizing a set of lamps and rejoicing in their light, and you wished to

make him truly happy, you would begin by blowing out all his lamps; and then throw open the shutters to let in the light of heaven.[55]

Father, when we like what is happening, gratitude comes more naturally, though even then we take far too much for granted. But when we do not understand your purposes, praise is an act of humble submission learned only through the experience of trials. Given the alternatives of bitterness, indifference, and praise, may we always choose to praise you. For whether or not we see your hand in all that is happening to us, you remain worthy of our praise. Someday, in retrospect, we, your children, will wonder how we ever could have doubted, how we ever could have failed to speak your praises. Give us today the same perspective we'll have one minute after we die.

69

True Wealth

These are the words of the Amen, the faithful and true witness, the ruler of God's creation. I know your deeds, that you are neither cold nor hot. I wish you were either one or the other! So, because you are lukewarm—neither hot nor cold—I am about to spit you out of my mouth. You say, "I am rich; I have acquired wealth and do not need a thing." But you do not realize that you are wretched, pitiful, poor, blind and naked....

Those whom I love I rebuke and discipline. So be earnest, and repent. Here I am! I stand at the door and knock. If anyone hears my voice and opens the door, I will come in and eat with him, and he with me.

To him who overcomes, I will give the right to sit with me on my throne, just as I overcame and sat down with my Father on his throne. He who has an ear, let him hear what the Spirit says to the churches.

—REVELATION 3:14–17, 19–22

I ndifference isn't better than sin; it *is* sin. Christ spits out of his mouth the spiritually apathetic who cling to the money idol and fail to recognize their need. Regardless of wealth, power, or status, apart from him our true state is one of being "wretched, pitiful, poor, blind and naked." He comes to the door of our hearts and knocks, inviting us to open it as we are, not as we pretend to be. Then, instead of punishing us for our arrogance, he comforts us in our shame. He will sit with us, eat with us, and, shockingly, make us fit to rule with him over a New Earth.

Will we come to Christ recognizing our utter spiritual bankruptcy so we can experience his grace? Or will we turn from him, convinced of our worthiness, so we'll face his wrath?

We come into this world needy, and we leave it the same way. Without suffering we would forget our neediness. If suffering seems too high a price for faith, it's because we underestimate faith's value.

Suffering uncovers our trust in God-substitutes and declares our need to transfer our trust to the only One who can bear its weight. Richard Baxter wrote, "Suffering so unbolts the door of the heart, that the Word hath easier entrance."[56] God uses suffering to bring us to the end of ourselves and back to Christ. And that is worth any cost.

Jesus said, "It is not the healthy who need a doctor, but the sick. I have not come to call the righteous, but sinners to repentance" (Luke 5:31–32). We need a cure, and that may require nasty-tasting medicine, painful surgery, and rigorous physical therapy.

My father, a Great Depression survivor, was a physically powerful and fiercely independent man. As he got older, his strength faded. He was then open to help from others—first from me, later from the

God he had adamantly rejected. I took him shopping and helped him in ways he'd never have accepted before. Age, weakness, and incapacity humbled this proud man—and his eternity will be dramatically better because of it.

C. S. Lewis said, "God whispers to us in our pleasures, speaks in our conscience, but shouts in our pains: it is His megaphone to rouse a deaf world."[57]

J. B. Phillips translates James 1:2–4, "When all kinds of trials and temptations crowd into your lives, my brothers, don't resent them as intruders, but welcome them as friends! Realise that they come to test your faith and to produce in you the quality of endurance. But let the process go on until that endurance is fully developed, and you will find you have become men of mature character, men of integrity with no weak spots."

How can we possibly obey this command to welcome difficulties instead of resenting them? By trusting that God tells the truth when he says these make us better people, increase our endurance, expand our ministry, and prepare us for eternal joy. If learning to trust God is good for us and God loves us enough to act for our good, why are we surprised when difficulties come?

Lord, you want us hot or cold, but not lukewarm. You are not content when we sit on the fence. You demand of us a decisive acceptance or rejection of who you are and what you have to offer. Thank you for disciplining our

indifference as you do our other sins. Show us our spiritual poverty; help us open our arms to release the idols we cling to that we might embrace your wealth. Help us to see that suffering can unbolt the doors of our hearts to give entrance to your Word.

70

Discipline's Good Fruit

Endure hardship as discipline; God is treating you as sons.
For what son is not disciplined by his father? If you are not
disciplined (and everyone undergoes discipline), then you
are illegitimate children and not true sons. Moreover, we
have all had human fathers who disciplined us and we
respected them for it. How much more should we submit
to the Father of our spirits and live! Our fathers disciplined
us for a little while as they thought best; but God disciplines
us for our good, that we may share in his holiness. No
discipline seems pleasant at the time, but painful. Later on,
however, it produces a harvest of righteousness and peace
for those who have been trained by it.

—HEBREWS 12:7–11

Often people tell me they want to write a book. Sometimes I tell
them, "What you really want is to *have written* a book." My
point is, that writing—at least the way I do it—involves a great deal
of hard work. Yes, at times I love it, I'm wired for it, but the research,

writing, rewriting, and editing require long hours, discipline, and sacrifices. Often I want to get up and do something else, anything else, but a deadline looms and I must complete the task.

Hard work is one meaning of discipline. Another is corrective discipline—imposing serious consequences for wrong choices. Yet another is maturing discipline, involving the assignment of heavy responsibilities in order to stretch one's capacity and increase willpower.

All forms of discipline are closely related; they each exert requirements on people that can serve to enhance their self-control, a virtue so highly regarded that it is also called a fruit of God's Spirit (Galatians 5:22).

In our side yard, a tree has survived ice storms, heavy snows, and howling winds. Several times in the thirty years we've lived here, I thought it would fall. Now I expect it to long outlast me. I've taken pictures of my preschool daughters in that tree and now of their children, my grandsons. It has lost many thick limbs, but others have grown, and harsh circumstances have made it stronger. In contrast, many protected and untested trees have long since fallen.

This tree has another secret. It lies at the lower part of our property, where rainwater sinks deep into the soil. This tree has all the nourishment it needs. The Bible says of the righteous man, "He is like a tree planted by streams of water, which yields its fruit in season and whose leaf does not wither. Whatever he does prospers" (Psalm 1:3).

Every champion will tell you that excellence comes out of disciplined training—and all training requires resistance. Without obstacles, we cannot build strength.

Not all discipline is designed to correct sin. Its purpose may be to cultivate righteousness. An athlete doesn't train just to fix a problem;

he trains *to improve his condition.* Hebrews 12:10 says, "God disciplines us for our good, that we may share in his holiness." Notice it does not say, "God disciplines us for his glory." That would have been perfectly true, of course. As his children, our good and God's glory are ultimately the same. But the point of the text is that it's in our best interests to become more Christlike.

The evils and suffering we may be called on to face are like steep hills that increase our spiritual lung capacity; resistance builds our endurance. Facing resistance is always hard. But it yields delayed gratification, as every athlete and farmer and writer will tell you. As Hebrews 12:11 says, "No discipline seems pleasant at the time, but painful. Later on, however, it produces a harvest of righteousness and peace for those who have been trained by it."

Let's be honest: virtually everyone who has suffered little in life is shallow, unmotivated, self-absorbed, and lacking in character. You know it and so do I. And yet we do everything we can to avoid challenges, both to our children and to ourselves. If we succeed in our avoidance, we'll develop in ourselves and our children the very kind of character we least admire.

God's parenting method doesn't shield us from adversity and the character it builds. We would do well to learn from him.

Lord, you constantly call us to be disciplined, to make short-term sacrifices that yield long-term benefits. You command us to abstain from impurity and gluttony and drunkenness, not to make our lives dull but to make them rich. You call

us to spend quality time with you, to pray, to share our faith, to make ethical decisions, and to prize and yield in our lives the fruit of the Spirit, including self-control. Graciously, you see to it that we reap what we sow, whether in punishment or reward. And you entrust us with responsibilities, including family and work and school and ministry, to stretch our abilities and develop our gifts and build our characters, to teach us to trust you for strength and wisdom that are beyond us. While no discipline is pleasant at the time, if we let it train us, it will always yield a harvest of peace and righteousness. Thank you.

71

Peace and Joy in Adversity

Rejoice in the Lord always. I will say it again: Rejoice! Let
your gentleness be evident to all. The Lord is near. Do not be
anxious about anything, but in everything, by prayer and
petition, with thanksgiving, present your requests to God.
And the peace of God, which transcends all understanding,
will guard your hearts and your minds in Christ Jesus.

—PHILIPPIANS 4:4–7

When he commands, "Rejoice in the Lord always," then
repeats it for emphasis, Paul can't be accused of being
unrealistic and out of touch with how difficult times can be. After all,
he wrote to the Philippians from prison! And not a prison with
lunchrooms, basketball hoops, and ESPN. If anyone had reason to be
resentful of his circumstances, Paul was that guy. He was a Roman
citizen, with all the rights and privileges thereof, yet was thrown in jail
just because he was telling people the truth about Jesus.

It's been said, "Bitterness is like drinking poison and waiting for the other person to die." In the face of evil and suffering, responding to God or others with bitterness, distrust, and accusations bears no good fruit. Instead, responding in honest brokenness and turning to God in submission, faith, and trust will yield untold riches of peace and comfort.

Christian slaves in nineteenth-century America sometimes were forbidden to sing. So when they went to the river for their chores, they would hang wet blankets around themselves, then fill water pots and sing into them to absorb the sound. They couldn't restrain their songs of praise. Those songs reflected deep sorrow and deep joy at the same time.

You may face evil or suffering to such a degree that you wonder if the God you love has turned his back on you. Your trial may last a day, a week, a year, a decade, or more. But I doubt your life will look worse than that of those Christian slaves. Stripped of liberty and dignity, with families routinely torn apart, they couldn't refrain from singing praises to God.

We would do well to spend our days preparing to worship God in hard times—those who have long lived in those times testify of a joy in their midst, as surely as slaves found joy in affliction.

Adversity itself doesn't cause our joy. Rather, our joy comes in the expectation of adversity's by-product, the development of godly character (see James 1:2–3 and Romans 5:3). God doesn't ask us to cheer because we lose our job or learn that a loved one has contracted cancer or our child has an incurable birth defect. He tells us to rejoice because he will produce in us something money can't buy and a life of ease will never produce—the precious quality of Christ-exalting perseverance.

God gives each of us a race to run. To finish well we must develop perseverance. The Christian life is not a hundred-meter dash but a marathon. Those who lack patience, endurance, and discipline will drop out of the race.

We should rejoice in suffering in the same way that Olympic athletes rejoice in their workouts—not because we find it easy, but because we know it will one day result in great reward. Like Jesus in Hebrews 12:1–2, we can rejoice now because of the eternal joy set before us.

Thank you, Father, for laying out for each of us a race, just as you did for the apostle Paul. Help us, as you helped Paul, to persevere, to run this marathon with endurance. Help us discipline ourselves and submit to the discipline of the life circumstances you've entrusted to us. Help us rejoice not merely when those circumstances please us, but even when they don't, because we know you are sovereign, all-knowing, and all-wise, because you have delivered us from Hell and promised us Heaven, because you are working together all things, even the worst things, for our good. Help us rejoice not merely as an exercise in positive thinking but because you have given us, in Christ, a rock-solid basis for rejoicing.

72

Only the Wounded Can Serve

> For I am already being poured out as a drink offering, and the
> time of my departure has come. I have fought the good fight, I
> have finished the race, I have kept the faith. Henceforth there
> is laid up for me the crown of righteousness, which the Lord,
> the righteous judge, will award to me on that Day, and not
> only to me but also to all who have loved his appearing.
> —2 TIMOTHY 4:6–8, ESV

Paul's letter to Timothy wasn't the first he wrote from prison in
Rome, it was his last. Final letter, final prison. The time of his
departure had come. It was to be an exodus not from life to death but
from death to life. He looked back at his life of service for Christ,
knowing he had fought hard and finished well. He'd been far from
perfect, yet he kept the faith. He knew a crown of righteousness
awaited him. Instead of leaving treasures behind, he was headed toward treasures in Heaven.

Soon the apostle's head would be cut off, by order of Emperor
Nero, the madman. Nero was the envy of the Earth; Paul the scum of

the Earth. Yet no one in his right mind would choose Nero's place over Paul's now because of what awaited them both in the afterlife. Paul was a wounded servant, but his wounds would be forever healed by the wounded Savior.

Paul's final words to Timothy reflect both his resolve and his tenderness. Suffering makes hearts tender and gives us greater love for others. Many physicians and nurses testify to this phenomenon when they return to their vocations after long periods of personal suffering. When they've been the patient, they grow far more sensitive to patients' needs.

A Thornton Wilder play called *The Angel That Troubled the Waters* is based loosely on John 5:1–4. A physician comes periodically to the pool of Bethesda, hoping to be the first in the moving water and so be healed of his depression.

One day the angel blocks the doctor from stepping into the water. "Draw back, physician," he commands, "this moment is not for you."

The man responds, "I pray thee, listen to my prayer."

"Healing is not for you," the angel insists.

The physician argues. "Surely, O Prince, you are not deceived by my apparent wholeness." He points out the terrible burden of his depression.

The angel assures him he knows of his affliction, then says to him, "Without your wound where would your power be? It is your very remorse that makes your low voice tremble into the hearts of men. The very angels themselves cannot persuade the wretched and blundering children on earth as can one human being broken on the wheels of living. In love's service only the wounded soldiers can serve. Draw back."

Later, the person who enters the pool first is healed and rejoices. He then turns to the physician and begs him to come to his home:

"My son is lost in dark thoughts. I—I do not understand him, and only you have ever lifted his mood.… My daughter, since her child has died, sits in the shadow. She will not listen to us but she will listen to you."[58]

Paul wrote, "Blessed be the God and Father of our Lord Jesus Christ, the Father of mercies and God of all comfort, who comforts us in all our affliction, so that we may be able to comfort those who are in any affliction, with the comfort with which we ourselves are comforted by God"(2 Corinthians 1:3–4, ESV).

Though a young woman exhibited joy in Christ despite her suffering, one particularly difficult day she asked her pastor why God hadn't let her die. He had no answer until a few days later when he met an unfamiliar couple at church. They told him about their visit with this woman in the hospital earlier that week, saying she had touched them on the deepest level. The young man said, "We went home and decided that we want to become Christians."[59]

So there came an answer to this dying woman's question: God had kept her alive to bring these people to Christ.

You don't have to see your child die or endure a divorce to offer comfort to someone who's suffered in those ways. You *must* have suffered, however. The résumé of every encourager and every counselor contains suffering.

Only the wounded can serve.

Lord, what a picture of Paul, sitting in that dark, damp, stinking prison cell while his soon-to-be assassin Nero lives

in unequaled opulence and luxury. Paul's conscience is clear, his life well-lived, while Nero's conscience is seared, his life corrupted. The pleasures of Heaven await the servant; the horrors of Hell await the tyrant. Thank you for this reminder not to waste our lives but to invest them in what will count for eternity. Lord, while you pour out your comfort to us directly by a ministry of your Holy Spirit, you are also fond of using people to comfort us. Thank you for the pleasure of both giving and receiving comfort in your family. Make me a servant, Lord. Help me see that my wounds are necessary because you use them to bring healing to others. Help me understand that you, my Servant King, will one day reward my humble service.

73

The Dawn of Hope

We did not follow cleverly invented stories when we told you about the power and coming of our Lord Jesus Christ, but we were eyewitnesses of his majesty. For he received honor and glory from God the Father when the voice came to him from the Majestic Glory, saying, "This is my Son, whom I love; with him I am well pleased." We ourselves heard this voice that came from heaven when we were with him on the sacred mountain.

And we have the word of the prophets made more certain, and you will do well to pay attention to it, as to a light shining in a dark place, until the day dawns and the morning star rises in your hearts.

—2 PETER 1:16–19

The words of God's prophets are a light from another world shining in this dark one. God calls us to live in their light until the eternal day dawns.

Despite present suffering, Scripture paints boldly across our lives the hope of promised resurrection, encouraging us to wait patiently, knowing it will come at just the right time.

To many of us, *hope* sounds wishful and tentative, but biblical hope means *to anticipate with trust.* We expect a sure thing, purchased on the Cross, accomplished and promised by an all-knowing God.

I spoke with a friend whose beloved wife was dying, leaving him and three teenage children behind. Weeping, he thanked God for his goodness in giving him an extra few months with his wife, painful as they were. In his brokenness he spoke of hanging on to the promise of resurrection. Wishful thinking? No. According to Scripture, his hope issues from a solidly grounded truth.

Dustin Shramek wrote about his son's death and how it affected him:

> My mother died when I was sixteen, two years after I had
> become a believer.... Having endured through her death I had
> come out on the other end with my faith intact and I again
> had hope that God was for me. After Owen died...while I
> certainly didn't feel joy, I knew that one day I would. The
> suffering I had endured through my mother's death had
> indeed produced hope.... I had experienced God's faithfulness
> and I knew that he would be faithful again.[60]

God remains faithful, of course, even when circumstances seem to say otherwise. Hope endures because God's promises remain true, no matter what.

In Tolkien's *The Return of the King,* Aragorn says, "Dawn is ever the hope of men." King David wrote, "Weeping may last for the night, but a shout of joy comes in the morning" (Psalm 30:5, NASB).

The night may seem long, but the truth is this: once morning comes, it will never end. Our suffering can be a source of hope for others. Though we are no substitute for God, we do serve as his ambassadors. I heard Christian counselor David Powlison say that although God alone is the blazing sun, we can be 3-watt night-lights. In darkness even a tiny light can bring hope.

Lord, thanks for the light of Heaven that shines out to us from your revealed Word. In this dark world, it's a lamp for our feet and a light for our paths. Help us immerse ourselves in your light and reflect it to others. As you are the blazing sun, give us power to be 3-watt night-lights. And if you can use hardship—or some less painful means—to increase our wattage for the good of others and for your glory, please do. And thanks for not asking our permission since we might have said no.

74

Worth the Price

Now I want you to know, brothers, that what has happened to me has really served to advance the gospel. As a result, it has become clear throughout the whole palace guard and to everyone else that I am in chains for Christ. Because of my chains, most of the brothers in the Lord have been encouraged to speak the word of God more courageously and fearlessly.

—Philippians 1:12–14

Paul rejoiced because his imprisonment served to advance the gospel. First, he reached an audience he otherwise couldn't have, including guards and prisoners. Second, his imprisonment emboldened his fellow Christians to speak God's Word. A third benefit, which he doesn't mention, is that being in prison restricted his activity, leaving him with more time to write a number of letters we might otherwise not have as part of God's Word.

Graham Staines and his wife, Gladys, left their home in Australia to minister to lepers in India—serving the poorest of the poor for thirty-four years.

At midnight on January 23, 1999, a mob of militant Hindus murdered Graham and his two sons, Phillip, age eleven, and Timothy, age six, by setting fire to the Jeep in which they slept.

In the most appalling way, Gladys and her daughter, Esther, found themselves alone. Their response to the tragedy appeared on the front page of every newspaper in India.

"I have only one message for the people of India." Gladys stunned the nation by saying, "I'm not bitter. Neither am I angry. But I have one great desire: That each citizen of this country should establish a personal relationship with Jesus Christ who gave his life for their sins.... Let us burn hatred and spread the flame of Christ's love. My husband and our children have sacrificed their lives for this nation; India is my home. I hope to be here and continue to serve the needy."

At the funeral, masses of people filled the streets—Hindus, Muslims, and Christians—to show respect for the Staines family and demonstrate solidarity against the killers.

After Gladys and her daughter, Esther, spoke at the conference where we met them, an Indian national leader told us about the impact of their response to the murders. He said the people of India asked, "Why would a man leave his wealthy country and serve lepers in India for thirty-four years? Why would his wife and daughter forgive the killers of their family? Why would they choose to stay and serve the poor? Who is this God they believe in? Could it be that all we've been told about Christians have been lies? Could it be that Jesus really is the truth?" He stated that many Hindus had come to faith in Christ through their witness.

The Staines family carried on a long tradition of God's people:

Others were tortured and refused to be released, so that they might gain a better resurrection. Some faced jeers and flogging, while still others were chained and put in prison. They were stoned; they were sawed in two; they were put to death by the sword. They went about in sheepskins and goatskins, destitute, persecuted and mistreated—*the world was not worthy of them.* (Hebrews 11:35–38)

The world needs more Christians bold enough to offer it not what it wants but what it needs.

Thank you, Lord, for a long history of advancing the gospel through your people's suffering. We're grateful not only for apostles and ancient martyrs but also for people like the Staines family, who have laid their lives on the line to bring the gospel of Jesus to the world. You have a special love for such servants. Help us follow their example and take up our crosses daily, making what are usually relatively small sacrifices to advance the gospel in our neighborhoods, communities, and workplaces.

75

A Higher Calling

Whatever happens, conduct yourselves in a manner worthy of the gospel of Christ. Then, whether I come and see you or only hear about you in my absence, I will know that you stand firm in one spirit, contending as one man for the faith of the gospel without being frightened in any way by those who oppose you. This is a sign to them that they will be destroyed, but that you will be saved—and that by God. For it has been granted to you on behalf of Christ not only to believe on him, but also to suffer for him, since you are going through the same struggle you saw I had, and now hear that I still have.

—PHILIPPIANS 1:27–30

God grants not only that we would believe in Christ but that we will suffer for him as well. Belief that requires no sacrifice is easy. To endure the suffering that comes from belief confirms belief's authenticity.

Joni Eareckson Tada spoke of a woman, pregnant with a disabled child, who cried out in desperation to her husband, "Things will never be the same." His response? "Maybe God doesn't *want* them to be the same."[61]

E. Stanley Jones wrote, "Don't bear trouble, use it. Take whatever happens—justice and injustice, pleasure and pain, compliment and criticism—take it up into the purpose of your life and make something out of it. Turn it into testimony."[62]

Richard Wurmbrand's *Tortured for Christ* influenced me profoundly as a young Christian. In Romania, guards tied prisoners to crosses and smeared them with excrement. From a human standpoint, the perpetrators seemed beyond redemption; yet some of the guards who did these unspeakable acts saw the inexplicable love, devotion, and faith of the Christians they tortured.

Wurmbrand wrote, "I have seen Christians in Communist prisons with fifty pounds of chains on their feet, tortured with red-hot iron pokers, in whose throats spoonfuls of salt had been forced, being kept afterward from water, starving, whipped, suffering from cold—and praying with fervor for the Communists."[63]

He told of guards coming to Christ while beating Christian prisoners, then confessing their faith and being imprisoned and tortured themselves.

When an African named Joseph heard about Jesus in a roadside conversation, he embraced him as Savior. Filled with excitement and joy, Joseph went door to door, telling his whole village about Jesus. To his amazement, his neighbors became violent. They beat him with strands of barbed wire and left him to die in the bush.

After days of passing in and out of consciousness, Joseph found the strength to get up. He decided he must have left something out of the good news or surely they would have accepted it. After rehearsing the message, Joseph limped back to the circle of huts and once more proclaimed Jesus.

Again they beat him, reopening his wounds. Joseph awoke in the wilderness, bruised, scarred—and determined to go back.

This time they attacked him even before he opened his mouth. As they flogged him, he spoke to them of Jesus. Before he passed out, he saw some of his female assailants begin to weep. When Joseph awoke, the ones who had so severely beaten him were trying to save his life. While he lay unconscious, the entire village had come to Christ.[64]

Romanian pastor Josef Tson—who had endured much in the hands of Romanian torturers—told me, "The gospel will *never* be spread without someone suffering."

Some readers of this book, or perhaps its writer, may be called not only to suffering but to martyrdom. It is not what we would seek, but if God chooses it for us, is there any higher calling?

Father, from its early days, the history of the gospel is a history of suffering. Seeing Christians willingly suffer for their Lord has drawn many to faith. Because the world crucified Jesus, it seems his followers should expect no less. But persecution is foreign to many of us—usually little more than raised eyebrows or looks of disapproval when we speak of Jesus. Give us courage, Lord, never to be ashamed to speak of a Savior who was not ashamed to die for us. And should you ordain our martyrdom, may we embrace it as a weighty privilege to be followed by eternal joy.

76

Tragedy Transformed

If you have any encouragement from being united with Christ, if any comfort from his love, if any fellowship with the Spirit, if any tenderness and compassion, then make my joy complete by being like-minded, having the same love, being one in spirit and purpose. Do nothing out of selfish ambition or vain conceit, but in humility consider others better than yourselves. Each of you should look not only to your own interests, but also to the interests of others.

Your attitude should be the same as that of Christ Jesus:
Who, being in very nature God,
did not consider equality with God something to be grasped,
but made himself nothing,
taking the very nature of a servant,
being made in human likeness.
And being found in appearance as a man,
he humbled himself
and became obedient to death—even death on a cross!
Therefore God exalted him to the highest place
and gave him the name that is above every name,

that at the name of Jesus every knee should bow,
    in heaven and on earth and under the earth,
and every tongue confess that Jesus Christ is Lord,
    to the glory of God the Father.
                —Philippians 2:1–11

No tragedy could be greater than God's blameless Son being slaughtered without mercy in horrid crucifixion. Yet as a result of his suffering, countless people will spend eternity with God in joyful celebration and endless pleasure. Jesus himself will be forever exalted, and all will recognize him as Lord, to the glory of God the Father. Eternal benefits are ours, all because he suffered.

For a number of years, Eric Liddell, the "Flying Scotsman" of the movie *Chariots of Fire* and Olympic gold medalist runner, served as a missionary in China. But when the Japanese occupation made life dangerous, he sent his pregnant wife and two daughters to Canada. Japanese invaders placed him in a squalid prison camp, where he lived several years before dying at age forty-three of a brain tumor. Liddell never saw his family again in this life. Upon learning of Eric's death, as it says at the end of *Chariots of Fire,* "All Scotland mourned."

Why did God withhold from this great man of faith a long life, years of fruitful service, the companionship of his wife, and the joy of raising those beloved children? It makes no sense.

And yet…

There is another way to look at the Eric Liddell story. Nanci and I discovered this firsthand twenty-some years ago while spending a day in England with Phil and Margaret Holder. Margaret was born in China to missionary parents. In 1939, when Japan took control of eastern China, soldiers separated thirteen-year-old Margaret from her parents and imprisoned her for six years.

Margaret told us many stories that day, several about a godly man who tutored her and the other children, organized sporting events, and brought God's Word to them. All the children in the camp loved him deeply. He was their inspiration. Margaret then told us this man's name: Eric Liddell. She had our attention!

Through fresh tears, Margaret said, "It was a cold February day when Uncle Eric died." If all Scotland mourned Liddell's death, no one mourned like the children in that camp. When five months later the children were rescued and reunited with their families, many of their stories were about Uncle Eric. Liddell's imprisonment broke the hearts of his family. But for years—nearly to the war's end—God used him as a lifeline to hundreds of children, including Margaret Holder.

Viewed from that perspective, the apparent tragedy of Liddell's presence in that camp makes more sense, doesn't it? I'm convinced Liddell and his family would tell us—and one day *will* tell us—that the sufferings of that time are not worthy to be compared with the glory they now know…and will forever know. A glory far greater than the suffering which achieved it.

If we can look at others' tragedies and see some divine purpose in them, it can help us believe that there is purpose in our tragedies too.

*God, you had profound purpose in the suffering of Jesus.
You had profound purpose in the suffering of Job and Joseph
and Eric Liddell and countless others. Give me the grace to
trust that you have profound purpose in the worst trial I or
my family and friends have ever faced and will ever face.
Once in your presence, we will know it to be true…but I
want to believe it now, with all my heart. Please help me to
believe.*

77

A Reason to Carry Our Cross

Then he said to them all: "If anyone would come after me, he must deny himself and take up his cross daily and follow me. For whoever wants to save his life will lose it, but whoever loses his life for me will save it. What good is it for a man to gain the whole world, and yet lose or forfeit his very self? If anyone is ashamed of me and my words, the Son of Man will be ashamed of him when he comes in his glory and in the glory of the Father and of the holy angels.…"

As they were walking along the road, a man said to him, "I will follow you wherever you go."

Jesus replied, "Foxes have holes and birds of the air have nests, but the Son of Man has no place to lay his head."

He said to another man, "Follow me."

But the man replied, "Lord, first let me go and bury my father."

Jesus said to him, "Let the dead bury their own dead, but you go and proclaim the kingdom of God."

Still another said, "I will follow you, Lord; but first let me go back and say good-by to my family."

Jesus replied, "No one who puts his hand to the plow and looks back is fit for service in the kingdom of God."

—LUKE 9:23–26, 57–62

Human nature hasn't changed in the slightest from the first century to the twenty-first. Christ still calls on people to follow him, and people still rationalize why now isn't a good time. Their reasons may appear to be sound, even compelling. But any reason not to follow Christ is a bad reason. Delayed obedience is disobedience.

Many of us have great ambitions. And we are perfectly willing to barter our souls to achieve them. But in the end, no matter what fleeting success we have gained, the price we pay will be too high. There are many things we can give our lives away for but only one that will return them to us in a far better condition.

Taking up our cross doesn't mean paying the price for our sins. God doesn't call us to repeat Christ's atonement but to accept it. He does call us to deny ourselves, make real though non-atoning sacrifices, and follow him (see Luke 9:23).

Taking up our crosses *daily* doesn't mean making one big once-and-for-all sacrifice and getting it over with. It means repeatedly, over and over again, day after day and year after year, saying no to present desires and plans in order to say yes to God and others. The good Samaritan cheerfully took up his cross by setting aside his schedule and commitments, giving his time and money to help the beaten man lying in the ditch (see Luke 10:25–37).

Elisabeth Elliot writes, "It is an unsettling business, this being made conformable to His death, and it cannot be accomplished without knocking out the props. If we understand that God is at work even when He knocks out the small props, it will not be so difficult for us to take when He knocks out bigger ones."[65]

We want deliverance from suffering. We don't want our loved ones to die. We don't want economic crises, job losses, marriage problems, errant children, car accidents, or cancer. Our prayers and often our expectations boil down to this: Jesus should make our lives go smoothly. That's what we want in a Messiah.

But it is not what *God* wants. Jesus is not our personal assistant charged with granting our wishes. While he sometimes doesn't give us what we want, he *always* gives us what we need.

Only when we regard suffering servanthood as our calling, as Jesus did, will we have the ability to face it as he did: "Consider him who endured such opposition from sinful men, so that you will not grow weary and lose heart" (Hebrews 12:3).

Through suffering we become powerless so that we might reach the powerless.

We like to serve from the power position. We'd rather be healthy, wealthy, and wise as we minister to the sick, poor, and ignorant. But people hear the gospel best when it comes from those who have known difficulty. If we preach God's Word yet have little personal familiarity with suffering, the credibility gap makes it difficult to speak into others' lives. But our suffering levels the playing field.

The God-man who died on the cross is best shared with others by those who also carry a cross. People will only see Jesus in us if we are like Jesus.

We choose some crosses to carry, Lord, and perhaps others we needlessly inflict on ourselves. But you appoint crosses to us, many not of our choosing. In each case, we cannot carry them without your help. We are too weak, too unwilling, too easily discouraged. We need a supernatural infusion of strength and an ability to endure, putting one foot in front of another, day after day. And in the midst of duty, we need joy, renewed hearts, living water that fills us to overflowing. Remind us that cross-carrying is a temporary death that leads to eternal life. Whatever we lose today in humble service to you, we will regain a trillion times over in the long tomorrow.

78

The Grand Reunion

"Behold, I am coming soon! My reward is with me, and I will give to everyone according to what he has done. I am the Alpha and the Omega, the First and the Last, the Beginning and the End.

"Blessed are those who wash their robes, that they may have the right to the tree of life and may go through the gates into the city. Outside are the dogs, those who practice magic arts, the sexually immoral, the murderers, the idolaters and everyone who loves and practices falsehood.

"I, Jesus, have sent my angel to give you this testimony for the churches. I am the Root and the Offspring of David, and the bright Morning Star."

The Spirit and the bride say, "Come!" And let him who hears say, "Come!" Whoever is thirsty, let him come; and whoever wishes, let him take the free gift of the water of life.

—REVELATION 22:12–17

J erry Hardin was my best friend from childhood. As kids, we went to movies at the Mt. Hood Theatre almost every Saturday. We fought armies and aliens in the fields around my house and slept outside in our sleeping bags with my golden retriever, Champ. Jerry and I went to school and played ball together, attended carnivals and parties together, and served as best man at each other's weddings. In high school we both came to faith in Christ, and our bond deepened.[66]

At age thirty-eight, Jerry was diagnosed with terminal cancer. He and I talked about suffering, healing, and Heaven. When it appeared God wasn't choosing to heal him, we talked about God's grace in giving him time to prepare for what awaits every one of us. He had time to talk with his wife and children. He'd lived well and didn't have to make many changes to be ready to die and meet his Creator.

Only a month before Jerry died, we played tennis together one last time. When I would lose a point, he'd accuse me of going easy on him. When I'd win one, he'd accuse me of taking advantage of a man dying of cancer. We laughed and kidded until we cried.

Jerry got steadily worse. I needed to head to the airport one Thursday morning, so I decided to leave home an hour early to see Jerry. My plan was to read to him the last two chapters of the Bible. As I read Revelation 21:4, God "will wipe every tear from their eyes," I looked up and saw tears falling from one of Jerry's eyes. I wiped them away.

I continued to read through my own tears, looking at Jerry between verses, right until Revelation 22:17: "The Spirit and the bride say, 'Come!' And let him who hears say, 'Come!' Whoever is thirsty, let him come; and whoever wishes, let him take the free gift of the water of life."

As I read the word *life,* I looked up, startled by what I saw. Jerry's body was vacant. Between the time I started reading that verse and the time I finished, my childhood friend had died.

The moment Jerry left, the room seemed utterly vacant. Jerry's wasted body was not what was left of him. It was simply what he left.

Jerry and I had attended our grade school and high school graduations together, celebrating afterward. And now, that day, I was with him again at his greatest graduation, from this life to the next.

Make no mistake. *Jerry* didn't come to an end. My friend simply left his temporary residence, relocating to a better place. His death didn't end our friendship; it only interrupted it. The friendship that began on Earth will resume and thrive in a far better world, the world for which God made us, a world of Christ-exalting wonders beyond our wildest dreams.

Thank you, King Jesus, for the price you paid to make that reunion happen!

Lord, please greet Jerry for me and tell him I'm looking forward to new adventures together, better than any of those great times we had here in the Shadowlands. But thank you for those times, because they were a gift from your hand. The nostalgia, the warmth in my heart, and the tears in my eyes as I am flooded with memories are just preparation for the unending joy to come—a joy that you speak of as your own when you say, as you already did to my friend Jerry, "Well done, my good and faithful servant. Enter into your Master's joy."

79

God's Call to Trust

Praise the LORD, O my soul;
    all my inmost being, praise his holy name.
Praise the LORD, O my soul,
    and forget not all his benefits—
who forgives all your sins
    and heals all your diseases,
who redeems your life from the pit
    and crowns you with love and compassion,
who satisfies your desires with good things
    so that your youth is renewed like the eagle's.
The LORD works righteousness
    and justice for all the oppressed....
He does not treat us as our sins deserve
    or repay us according to our iniquities.
For as high as the heavens are above the earth,
    so great is his love for those who fear him;
as far as the east is from the west,
    so far has he removed our transgressions from us.
As a father has compassion on his children,
    so the LORD has compassion on those who fear him....

But from everlasting to everlasting
    the LORD's love is with those who fear him,
    and his righteousness with their children's children—
with those who keep his covenant
    and remember to obey his precepts.
The LORD has established his throne in heaven,
    and his kingdom rules over all.…
Praise the LORD, all his works
    everywhere in his dominion.
Praise the LORD, O my soul.

      —PSALM 103:1–6, 10–13, 17–19, 22

God does not only rule over Heaven. He rules over all. There is no end to his dominion. Abraham Kuyper, who was both a great theologian and prime minister of the Netherlands, put it this way: "There is not one inch in the entire area of our human life about which Christ, who is Sovereign of all, does not cry out, 'Mine!'"

Part of not forgetting God's benefits is recognizing his kindness and wisdom in what he sovereignly permits and what he does not.

Suffering is limited. It could be far worse.

Suffering is temporary. It could last far longer.

Suffering, as we've seen, produces some desirable good. It can make us better people, and it can reveal God's character in ways that bring him glory and bring us good.

God can see all the ultimate results of suffering; we can see only some. When we see more, in his presence, we will forever praise him for it. He calls upon us to trust him and begin that praise now.

According to Psalm 103, the sovereign God looks upon us with an amazing and expansive love: "For as high as the heavens are above the earth, so great is his love for those who fear him; as far as the east is from the west, so far has he removed our transgressions from us."

But how can an infinitely holy God remove our transgressions from us? Jesus Christ, God's Son, in a supreme act of love, became a man to deliver us from sin and suffering (see John 3:16). Jesus lived a sinless life (see Hebrews 2:17–18; 4:15–16). He died to pay the penalty for our sins (see 2 Corinthians 5:21). On the cross, he took upon himself the Hell we do deserve in order to purchase for us the Heaven we don't deserve. At his death he said, "It is finished" (John 19:30), using the Greek word for canceling certificates of debt—meaning "paid in full." Jesus then rose from the grave, defeating sin and conquering death (see 1 Corinthians 15:3–4, 54–57). That's the truth.

Christ offers freely the gift of forgiveness and eternal life: "Whoever is thirsty, let him come; and whoever wishes, let him take the free gift of the water of life" (Revelation 22:17).

Is God drawing you to himself right now? If you have not accepted this gift purchased by Christ at such a great price to him, what's stopping you?

Thank you, Father, that there is nothing cold and distant about your sovereignty. It is warmed by your love and

affection, as demonstrated in the Incarnation and Atonement. What amazing lengths you went to in order to save us from our sin, removing it completely, as far as the east is from the west. Thank you that every square inch of the cosmos is indeed yours, and after the final judgment you will transform every millimeter of it into a redeemed state. How amazing not just that you will do it but that you promise your children we will be there to see it!

80

God's Tears

On his arrival, Jesus found that Lazarus had already been in the tomb for four days.... When Martha heard that Jesus was coming, she went out to meet him.... Jesus said to her, "Your brother will rise again.... I am the resurrection and the life. He who believes in me will live, even though he dies; and whoever lives and believes in me will never die. Do you believe this?"

"Yes, Lord," she told him.... And after she had said this, she went back and called her sister Mary aside. "The Teacher is here," she said, "and is asking for you." When Mary heard this, she got up quickly and went to him....

When Mary reached the place where Jesus was and saw him, she fell at his feet and said, "Lord, if you had been here, my brother would not have died."

When Jesus saw her weeping...he was deeply moved in spirit and troubled. "Where have you laid him?" he asked.

"Come and see, Lord," they replied.

Jesus wept.

Then the Jews said, "See how he loved him!"...

Jesus, once more deeply moved, came to the tomb. It was a cave with a stone laid across the entrance. "Take away the stone," he said....

So they took away the stone....

Jesus called in a loud voice, "Lazarus, come out!" The dead man came out, his hands and feet wrapped with strips of linen, and a cloth around his face.

Jesus said to them, "Take off the grave clothes and let him go."

—JOHN 11:17, 20, 23, 25–29, 32–36,
38–39, 41, 43–44

Jesus knew he was going to raise Lazarus twice. Once—that very day—to resume a mortal life, and then when Lazarus would die again another day. Lazarus's second raising, into an undying resurrection body, will happen along with our resurrection.

God does not look fondly upon death. It wasn't part of his original design but came from sin and the Curse. Death caused Jesus to weep. His heart broke for the broken hearts of his beloved Mary and Martha. At the time, his own death already loomed large, placing a terrible burden upon him. While he knew what awaited him in Heaven, he also knew that before enjoying Heaven's comfort and glory, he must walk through a dark valley more excruciating than anyone before or after him would ever walk.

The shortest verse in the English Bible is "Jesus wept" (John 11:35). It's the easiest memory verse, yet a very worthy one. If we ever question whether God understands or whether he cares, those two words are our unequivocal answer: Jesus wept. The Savior sobbed. Messiah moaned. God shed tears. What more proof of God's heart and emotions and care and understanding do we want?

Job, in his suffering, was mainly silent for at least a week before pouring forth his sorrows and complaints like a fire hose. Then he proceeded to share everything on his mind, which included nothing God didn't already know.

Just as God knew exactly how Job felt before he said a word, so God knows how you feel and what you're thinking. When you pretend you don't feel hurt or angry or devastated, you're not fooling God. Be honest!

Don't misunderstand; I am *not* encouraging you to be angry at God or to blame him. He deserves no blame. Rather, I am encouraging you to honestly confess to God your feelings of hurt, resentment, and anger.

Often we look at suffering from our perspective and forget that God sees from another vantage point. Our friend Patti Franklin wrote of life during the early years of her husband John's paralysis. Try to look at her words from God's perspective, imagining what they mean to him:

> I never once saw myself as strong, but weak and bewildered
> and afraid. But I remembered that God was strong and He
> was able, so I hung on to Him for dear life. Some of my
> prayers were along the line of "God, help me. Help John. Help
> our children." I would talk to Him as I drove back and forth
> to the hospital and at night and basically all the time.

The worse things got for us, the more clearly we could see His beauty and goodness. The better we could see how worthy He was of our worship and how tenderly He cared for us and helped us.[67]

God promises in Hebrews 13:5, "Never will I leave you; never will I forsake you." The original Greek here is full of emphatic negatives. Kenneth Wuest translates it, "I will not, I will not cease to sustain and uphold you. I will not, I will not, I will not let you down."[68]

David asked God, "Record my lament; list my tears on your scroll—are they not in your record?" (Psalm 56:8). David believed his suffering mattered, that God counted it as precious, so precious that the Lord kept an account of every tear.

This gives special meaning to the promise that God will wipe away every tear from his children's eyes (see Revelation 21:4). Our tears are all recorded in Heaven's books. God is keeping track of the pain behind each and will deal with them one by one. And remember, this is a God who not only made tear ducts but who has them. Jesus, the second member of the triune God, is also a man, and as the God-man he shed tears.

When God wipes away all our tears with his gentle, omnipotent hand, I believe our eyes will fall on the scars that made our suffering his so that his eternal joy could become ours.

Father, it makes all the difference in the world to me that you don't just understand my pain because you know every-

thing, but that you understand because you walked this world. You wept over the death of a friend. You sweated drops of blood while anticipating the horrors of your imminent death, and you chose to die for my sins when you could have called down a vast army of angels to stop it all from happening. Help me begin to grasp how utterly unthinkable, how truly amazing this is. And if I am ever tempted to accuse you or resent you or question you, remind me that Jesus wept. Jesus died. Jesus lives. Jesus cares. Jesus returns.

81

Fulfilled Hope

Hope deferred makes the heart sick,
   but a longing fulfilled is a tree of life.
            —PROVERBS 13:12

Never be lacking in zeal, but keep your spiritual fervor, serving the Lord. Be joyful in hope, patient in affliction, faithful in prayer.
            —ROMANS 12:11–12

May the God of hope fill you with all joy and peace as you trust in him, so that you may overflow with hope by the power of the Holy Spirit.
            —ROMANS 15:13

Hope is a much stronger word in the Bible than it is for most of us today. The hope of deliverance and resurrection is based solidly on the promise of an almighty truth-telling, covenant-keeping God who never fails and is never thwarted, who *always* keeps his promises. Whenever we hope for what God has promised, we don't wish for a possibility; we anticipate a certainty.

Researchers conducted a study on stress with Israeli soldiers. They assured one group that the march would end at a certain point but kept the other group in the dark. Although both groups marched an identical distance, those who didn't know how long they would march registered a much higher level of stress. Why? Because they had no hope, no tangible assurance that the forced march would end. They felt helpless, wondering when, or if, they could ever rest.

Hope points to the light at the end of life's tunnel. It not only makes the tunnel endurable, it fills the heart with anticipation of what's at the other end: a world alive, fresh, beautiful, and without pain, suffering, or war. A world without disease, without accident, without tragedy. A world without dictators or madmen. A world ruled by the only One worthy of ruling (see Revelation 5:12). Though we don't know exactly *when,* we do know for sure that either by our deaths or by Christ's return, our suffering *will* end. From before the beginning, God drew the line in eternity's sand to say for his children, "*This much and no more,* then endless joy."

Suffering is God's invitation to look to Jesus and look forward to Heaven. The answer to the problem of evil is a person and a place. Jesus is the person. Heaven is the place. No one else and nowhere else will satisfy.

I spent three hours with Carol King, a godly woman in her fifties who was dying of cancer. She'd read a few of my books and wanted to talk about Heaven. What struck me that day was the gift of laughter.

"I need some new clothes," Carol said, "but why buy them? I used to get jumbo-sized shampoo, but now it's a waste. I don't even buy green bananas, because by the time they ripen I'll probably be gone!" Carol said it not morbidly but with heartfelt peace and joy. She anticipated a better world. Carol had already suffered great pain and had no romantic notions about death. But she faced death with quiet joy and contagious laughter.

I left, encouraged by a dying woman I'll always consider my friend. She went to her Savior soon after. I look forward to laughing with Carol in the world where Jesus promised those now weeping, "You will laugh" (Luke 6:21).

My anticipation, by the way, is not wishful thinking. Since God is the Almighty promise keeper who never lies and knows the end from the beginning, I am looking forward to a certainty.

Lord, remind us that our calling is not to wish for the best but to trust the utter faithfulness of an all-powerful, promise-keeping God who always has a purpose and a plan, who ordained from eternity past every moment of time and all the ages yet to unfold. As your magnificent story of redemption moves to culmination, thank you not only for writing the chapters yet to come but for also revealing some of their content, enough that we may know the solid certainty of a New Heaven and New Earth over which the risen Christ will reign, with your resurrected children beside you, worshiping and serving you in a world forever free of curse and suffering and death. Thank you for this promise—not merely my wish but a blood-bought certainty.

82

Nourishment for the Soul

Your word is a lamp to my feet
    and a light for my path.
I have taken an oath and confirmed it,
    that I will follow your righteous laws.
I have suffered much;
    preserve my life, O LORD, according to your word.
Accept, O LORD, the willing praise of my mouth,
    and teach me your laws.
Though I constantly take my life in my hands,
    I will not forget your law.
The wicked have set a snare for me,
    but I have not strayed from your precepts.
Your statutes are my heritage forever;
    they are the joy of my heart.
My heart is set on keeping your decrees
    to the very end.

—PSALM 119:105–112

The psalmist states, "I have suffered much." The God to whom he prays knows how much and the nature of his suffering. He knows the same about us but invites us to pour out our hearts to him nevertheless.

God's Word gives us strength in our weariness, and it comforts and sustains us. When not afflicted, we tend to go astray, but God uses our afflictions to help us obey his Word. Without God's Word to sustain us, we will perish in our affliction. God has purpose in our affliction, and one purpose is to know him better through studying his Word. We must not forget God's Word, for it preserves our lives. His Word is a source of delight to us.

Clearly, if we are to face suffering well, if we are not to waste our suffering, we must let it take us to God's Word. If we don't, our loss will be incalculable. If we do, our gain will be abundant and eternal.

I love to look at the books on people's shelves. One night when Nanci and I were at Ken and Joni Tada's home, I looked through the bookshelves, lined with classic works by great theologians and preachers, including many of my favorites, such as Charles Spurgeon. The books Joni reads are rich and deep, centered in God's Word, food for her soul. No wonder both the life she lives and the books she writes share those same qualities.

I've made a habit of reading books by men and women who point me to God's book. As a young Christian, I loved the writings of Joseph Bayly. Joe and his wife lost three of their children—one at eighteen days, after surgery; another at five years, from leukemia; and a third at eighteen years, in a sledding accident (and complicated by hemophilia).

In 1969, the year I came to Christ, Joe wrote a little book called

Psalms of My Life. It contained a poem that, forty years later, still touches me. It's called "A Psalm While Packing Books."

This cardboard box
Lord
see it says
Bursting limit
100 lbs. per square inch.
The box maker knew
how much strain
the box would take
what weight
would crush it.
You are wiser
than the box maker
maker of my spirit
my mind
my body.
Does the box know
when pressure increases close to
the limit?
No
It knows nothing.
But I know
when my breaking point
Is near.
And so I pray
Maker of my soul

Determiner of the pressure
within
upon
me
Stop it
lest I be broken
Or else
change the pressure rating
of this fragile container
of your grace
so that I may bear more.[69]

Before difficult times come your way, develop habits of studying God's Word, listening to Christ-centered teaching and music, and reading soul-nourishing literature, both nonfiction and fiction. Daily fill the reservoir from which you can draw when facing difficult times—and helping others face theirs.

Great peace comes in meditating on the attributes of our God and his care for us.

Thank you, Lord, for knowing our limits and knowing the proper arrangement of the weight and quantity of our suffering. God, as we face our affliction, take us deep into your Word. Let us not be content with empty entertainment and diversions to numb our pain. Your Word doesn't numb us; instead it makes us alive, energizes us, strengthens and sus-

tains us, and comforts us with truth. It confronts sin in our lives, encourages our obedience, and gives us delight in you. Who but the devil and sin itself would distract us from such treasure? Change our habits of leisure, Lord. Prompt us to abandon entertainment that scorns and violates your Word, to listen to music that celebrates your Word, and to embrace great Scripture-saturated books that lead us to you and your Word. Remind us that your Word is the source of correction, training, eternal perspective, and joyful rest from weariness and sorrow.

83

Temporary Darkness, Eternal Light

He parted the heavens and came down;
>   dark clouds were under his feet.
He mounted the cherubim and flew;
>   he soared on the wings of the wind.
He made darkness his covering, his canopy around him—
>   the dark rain clouds of the sky.
Out of the brightness of his presence clouds advanced,
>   with hailstones and bolts of lightning.
The LORD thundered from heaven;
>   the voice of the Most High resounded....
He reached down from on high and took hold of me;
>   he drew me out of deep waters.
He rescued me from my powerful enemy,
>   from my foes, who were too strong for me....
He brought me out into a spacious place;
>   he rescued me because he delighted in me....
The LORD has rewarded me according to my righteousness,
>   according to the cleanness of my hands in his sight.

To the faithful you show yourself faithful,
    to the blameless you show yourself blameless,
to the pure you show yourself pure,
    but to the crooked you show yourself shrewd.
You save the humble
    but bring low those whose eyes are haughty.
You, O LORD, keep my lamp burning;
    my God turns my darkness into light.

        —PSALM 18:9–13, 16–17, 19, 24–28

God is portrayed in Scripture as full of light. He has a bright radiance, seen by Moses and Elijah and Isaiah and the apostle John and shown in Christ at the Transfiguration. The apostle John is emphatic: "God is light; in him there is no darkness at all" (1 John 1:5).

Psalm 18 speaks of "the brightness of his presence," yet paradoxically also speaks of him coming down from the heavens with "dark clouds" under his feet. We're told of God that "he made darkness his covering, his canopy around him—the dark rain clouds of the sky." How do dark clouds fit with the brightness of the noonday sun? Somehow it relates to the fallen human condition and the difficulty of seeing the full light of God's presence in a world still under the Curse.

While I don't suffer chronic depression, I've had a few periods of several months of depression that have awakened me to its reality and the hold it can take. A novelist friend wrote me:

I pleaded with God for healing and understanding. I thought if I could just understand it, I'd somehow solve it.

Never, in all my years of being a Christian, did I cling to God so closely. Never had I talked to Him so honestly. Those weeks, months, and even years of questioning and searching drew me nearer to Him. Walking through my discontent led me to a life so much richer than the one I'd been living. God used my depression and pain for something so much greater than I could envision. I've learned that there is purpose in struggle...even when we can't see it.

When I posted a blog about a time of depression I was experiencing, a few people expressed shock that someone who had written about subjects such as grace and Heaven could ever be depressed! I had to laugh, since far better people than I have experienced far worse depression—Charles Spurgeon, Martin Luther, John Owen, and William Cowper, to name a few.

Some depression comes from simply feeling the crushing weight of pain and brokenness in one's life and the lives of others around the globe. Of course, self-preoccupied woe-is-me depression quickly becomes deeply unhealthy. But sometimes when we feel burdened, we may simply be joining the whole of creation in groaning because of a suffering world. In that case, we're in good company, for "the Spirit himself intercedes for us with groans that words cannot express" (Romans 8:26).

It's no sin to feel that burden, and sometimes it's a sin *not* to. Some of what passes for Christian contentment is, in fact, apathy toward the plight of God's image-bearers. Our lives should reflect a groaning that gives way to joy, celebrating what God has done for us in Christ and thanking him that he will rescue us once and for all from evil and suffering.

Helen Keller, blind and deaf since a toddler, wrote, "Although the world is full of suffering it is also full of the overcoming of it.… Believe, when you are most unhappy, that there is something for you to do in the world. So long as you can sweeten another's pain, life is not in vain."[70]

Psalm 18, after speaking of both light and darkness, ends beautifully: "You, O LORD, keep my lamp burning; my God turns my darkness into light."

The darkness of the soul will not go on unbroken in this life. But even if it did, the bright light of the New Heaven and the New Earth is coming, so close that even now it is almost within reach: "The city does not need the sun or the moon to shine on it, for the glory of God gives it light, and the Lamb is its lamp" (Revelation 21:23).

Lord, rescue us from the darkness of sin, and shine upon us the light of forgiveness. But rescue us too from the dark night of the soul that sometimes falls upon even the righteous, who confess their sins and seek your face yet still walk under a gloomy cloud of depression. Reassure us that we are in good company, for many of your great saints have so suffered. Lord, help us trust you until the darkness lifts. But please break through it and be pleased to shine upon us— not just in eternity but even now—the light of joy.

84

Grace for Living

Therefore, prepare your minds for action; be self-controlled; set your hope fully on the grace to be given you when Jesus Christ is revealed. As obedient children, do not conform to the evil desires you had when you lived in ignorance. But just as he who called you is holy, so be holy in all you do; for it is written: "Be holy, because I am holy."

Since you call on a Father who judges each man's work impartially, live your lives as strangers here in reverent fear. For you know that it was not with perishable things such as silver or gold that you were redeemed from the empty way of life handed down to you from your forefathers, but with the precious blood of Christ, a lamb without blemish or defect. He was chosen before the creation of the world, but was revealed in these last times for your sake. Through him you believe in God, who raised him from the dead and glorified him, and so your faith and hope are in God.

—1 Peter 1:13–21

God has redeemed us through his grace in the past and empowers us with his grace in the present. But he tells us to fix our hearts on future grace: "Set your hope fully on the grace to be given you when Jesus Christ is revealed."

Joni Eareckson Tada writes:

"O God," I often pray in the morning, "God, I cannot do this. I cannot do this thing called quadriplegia…. I have no smile for this woman who's going to walk into my bedroom in a moment. She could be having coffee with another friend, but she's chosen to come here to help me get up. O God, please may I borrow your smile?"[71]

Twenty-five years ago, my friend Roger Huntington was a successful Alaskan businessman, bank director, and chairman of the board of a $200 million corporation.

In 1988, Roger's plane crashed. The fuel tank cover dislodged, and gasoline poured on his head. A fire burned 60 percent of his body, permanently marring his face.

The first time Roger saw himself sideways in a mirror, he wept. He asked God why. He contemplated suicide but refused to do it because he knew the pain it would inflict on others.

Roger realized that all he had depended on had disappeared. Since then, he has developed character and touched many lives through his response to great suffering. Roger considers his scars a tribute to human weakness. But he says those scars are also "a testimony to God's healing power."

Joni Tada speaks of the humble and afflicted:

They are people who are humiliated by their weaknesses.
Catheterized people whose leg bags spring leaks on somebody
else's brand-new carpet. Immobilized people who must be fed,
cleansed, dressed, and taken care of like infants. Once-active
people crippled by chronic aches and pains....

   It is when your soul has been blasted bare, when you feel
raw and undone, that you can be better bonded to the Savior.
And then you not only meet suffering on God's terms, but
you meet joy on God's terms. And then God—as he does
every morning at 7:30 when I cry out to him out of my
affliction—happily shares his gladness, his joy flooding over
heaven's walls filling my heart in a waterfall of delight, which
then in turn always streams out to others in a flood of
encouragement, and then erupts back to God in an ecstatic
fountain of praise. He gets your heart pumping for heaven. He
injects his peace, power, and perspective into your spiritual
being. He imparts a new way of looking at your hardships. He
puts a song in your heart.[72]

*God, put a song in the hearts of your people burdened by
ravages of the Curse. We want to set our hopes on the grace
that will be revealed to us when your Son returns to this
Earth to set up his kingdom. But sometimes that seems too*

far away. We need your grace today, this moment, to know that we are in your hands, that you will get us through. Thank you for your past grace poured out for us on the cross and your future grace that will be poured out to us in your eternal kingdom. Give us present grace, that we may sing your praises now.

85

Grace for Dying

Since the children have flesh and blood, [Jesus] too shared in their humanity so that by his death he might destroy him who holds the power of death—that is, the devil—and free those who all their lives were held in slavery by their fear of death. For surely it is not angels he helps, but Abraham's descendants. For this reason he had to be made like his brothers in every way, in order that he might become a merciful and faithful high priest in service to God, and that he might make atonement for the sins of the people. Because he himself suffered when he was tempted, he is able to help those who are being tempted.

—HEBREWS 2:14–18

The miracle of the Cross was made possible by the miracle of the Incarnation. The angels must have been stunned to see the second member of the triune God descend to Earth and become a human being. The baby born in that Bethlehem barn was God, and he was born in order to die. His death delivered us from Hell at death, and therefore delivered us from what causes us to fear death. But while his suffering on the cross atoned for our sins, his suffering, tests, and temptations allowed him to understand and empathize with us and help us.

Some people hold tenaciously to a faith that their child will not die, that their cancer will disappear, that their spouse will recover from a stroke. Do they have faith in God, or is their faith in what they desperately want God to do?

Shadrach, Meshach, and Abednego refused to worship an idol even though King Nebuchadnezzar threatened to throw them into a blazing furnace:

> O Nebuchadnezzar, we do not need to defend ourselves
> before you in this matter. If we are thrown into the blazing
> furnace, the God we serve is able to save us from it, and he
> will rescue us from your hand, O king. But even if he does
> not, we want you to know, O king, that we will not serve
> your gods or worship the image of gold you have set up.
> (Daniel 3:16–18)

God sometimes chooses to heal in supernatural answer to prayer. Still, all who pray for healing should affirm, like Daniel's friends, that they will worship and honor and obey God "even if he does not."

Emmanuel Ndikumana was nineteen years old when he heard that a group of young men in Burundi planned to murder him in two weeks. He chose to stay where he was and survived the attempted murder through God's amazing providence. Emmanuel made this enlightening comment: "You Americans have a strange attitude toward death; you act as if it is the end."

While reading one chapter a day from my book *Heaven,* a man and his dying wife spent her last forty-six days talking openly about her eternal future. This allowed them to cry and laugh together. After reading the final chapter, they prayed and then she died. He called their final days together precious.

Think of how different that time would have been if one of them had refused to accept her impending death. We associate fighting death with courage, and sometimes that's true. At other times there is greater courage in accepting a death and preparing for it. At memorial services, no one says, "I was very touched when my Dad maintained a cheerful attitude after getting that big promotion."

But they do say, "Dad modeled trust in God by cheerfully serving him in his dying days." Although death is the last enemy, the ghastly result of the Fall and the Curse, Christ made death a passageway into the loving presence of God.

Christ has liberated us from the need to fear death!

Lord, thank you for defusing the greatest reason to fear death. While we should rightly fear Hell, by purchasing us Heaven you changed our destiny and gave us cause to look forward to what we will discover on the other side of death. It is now a doorway to the place for which we were made. God, help your people never to act as if death is the end.

86

No More Good-Byes

Since, then, you have been raised with Christ, set your hearts on things above, where Christ is seated at the right hand of God. Set your minds on things above, not on earthly things. For you died, and your life is now hidden with Christ in God. When Christ, who is your life, appears, then you also will appear with him in glory.

— COLOSSIANS 3:1–4

We are so closely linked with our Redeemer, who is in Heaven, that we in some real sense have been raised with him. We are to set our hearts not only on Christ but on the place where he is and where we will go at our deaths. When Christ returns to set up his kingdom, to bring Heaven down to Earth, we will be right there with him, sharing in his glory.

When we grasp this reality, it should transform our view of death. We shouldn't obsess over it. Neither should we follow our culture's lead in denying death until it thrusts itself upon us. When we fail to face death, we remain unprepared for what awaits us on the other side.

Death isn't the worst that can happen to us; on the contrary, for God's children, death leads to the best. Paul says, "For to me, to live is Christ and to die is gain.... I desire to depart and be with Christ, which is better by far" (Philippians 1:21, 23). Lest we think he was speaking purely by faith, the truth is that Paul himself had actually been taken into Heaven years before writing those words (2 Corinthians 12:1–6). He knew firsthand what awaited him in Paradise. He wasn't speculating when he called it gain. To be in the very presence of Jesus, enjoying the wonders of his being, to be with God's people and no longer subject to sin and suffering? "Better by far" is an understatement!

Of course, death is not a natural part of life as God intended it. It is the unnatural result of evil. And yet God has removed the ultimate sting of death, which explains the appropriate sense of peace and triumph that accompanies grief at a Christian's memorial service.

"Brothers, we do not want you to be ignorant about those who fall asleep, or to grieve like the rest of men, who have no hope" (1 Thessalonians 4:13). We grieve differently, yet honestly and openly, precisely because we look forward to a New Heaven and a New Earth (see 2 Peter 3:13).

I've conducted funerals for both Christians and non-Christians. As I look into the eyes of those gathered, the tears are just as real for Christians, but I also see hope, perspective, and peace in the midst of their mourning. We haven't lost our believing loved ones—we know where they are. And we know that in the resurrection we will live with God and with them on a New Earth.

For Christians, death is not a wall but a doorway. Death is not a last good-bye but a "See you later." When my mother died, it felt like part of me went to Heaven with her.

After Mom's death, I returned from my parents' house at 3:00 a.m. and woke Karina. I asked my groggy not-quite-three-year-old daughter, "Do you know where Grandma Alcorn is right now?"

Karina smiled and said, "Yes, Daddy—*she's in Heaven.*"

I stared at her, stunned. Her grandmother, with whom Karina was very close, had been in bed at her own house for the previous two months. How did my daughter know she'd gone to Heaven? I'm convinced God told Karina as she slept.

While we should never pray to our loved ones, only to God, I've often asked God to give my mom a hug or tell her I love her. It's part of anticipating our reunion. And that reunion I so greatly anticipate won't take place—unless Christ returns before then—until I die.

Father, I don't look forward to the process of dying, but I do look forward to the end result—being with you and with so many I love who have left this world over the years, not to mention all the new friends I'll be making. I don't want to leave my family and friends who are here, but all of them who love you are certain to follow, and that is wonderful beyond words. But no friendship, Lord, will mean as much as yours. Help me set my eyes on Jesus, the person for whom I was made, and Heaven, the place for which I was made. The grand reunion awaits. Thank you that every day brings it one day closer.

87

The Long Tomorrow

For this reason, since the day we heard about you, we have not stopped praying for you and asking God to fill you with the knowledge of his will through all spiritual wisdom and understanding. And we pray this in order that you may live a life worthy of the Lord and may please him in every way: bearing fruit in every good work, growing in the knowledge of God, being strengthened with all power according to his glorious might so that you may have great endurance and patience, and joyfully giving thanks to the Father, who has qualified you to share in the inheritance of the saints in the kingdom of light. For he has rescued us from the dominion of darkness and brought us into the kingdom of the Son he loves, in whom we have redemption, the forgiveness of sins.

—COLOSSIANS 1:9–14

God has made us his children and qualified us to share in the eternal inheritance that awaits us in his kingdom. He rescued us from the kingdom of darkness and transferred our citizenship to the kingdom of light. It doesn't get any better than that!

Many who receive a terminal diagnosis experience for the first time the bittersweet blessing of coming to terms with their mortality.

When our friend Leona Bryant discovered she had a short time to live, she told me of her radical change in perspective. "The most striking thing," she said, "is that I find myself totally uninterested in all the conversations about material things. Things used to matter to me, but now I find my thoughts are never on possessions, but always on Christ and people. I consider it a privilege to live each day knowing I'll die soon. What a difference it makes!"

Leona had her eyes on the prize of her eternal inheritance in the kingdom of light. In comparison, nothing here in the Shadowlands could hold her interest.

All of us should live our short todays in light of what A. W. Tozer called "the long tomorrow." None of us knows the time or place of our death. Neither can we know its manner. And there's nothing we can do to escape it: "No man has power over the wind to contain it; so no one has power over the day of his death" (Ecclesiastes 8:8). The statistic never wavers: 100 percent of people die.

Wise people live in light of death's certainty. In the oldest psalm, Moses wrote, "The length of our days is seventy years—or eighty, if we have the strength; yet their span is but trouble and sorrow, for they quickly pass, and we fly away…. Teach us to number our days aright, that we may gain a heart of wisdom" (Psalm 90:10, 12).

Christians get two opportunities to live on Earth. This first one begins and ends. It is but a dot. The second opportunity will be an infinite line, extending into forever. We all live *in* the dot. If we're wise, we'll live *for* the line. "In keeping with his [God's] promise we are looking forward to a new heaven and a new earth, the home of righteousness" (2 Peter 3:13).

Two things stand between where we live now and that marvelous world where we'll live forever: death and resurrection. If we never died, we'd never be resurrected. We'd never enjoy a glorious eternity with Christ and our spiritual family.

So while death is an enemy and part of sin's curse, because of Christ's death and resurrection, it's the dark passage through which we enter the brilliance of our inheritance: never-ending life in God's magnificent kingdom.

Thank you, Lord, for the inheritance you're preparing for your children. You have a world in mind for us to rule. Help us never to be content with this lesser world that groans under the Curse. As you did with my friend Leona, move our hearts and conversations away from the temporary and toward the eternal.

88

"Welcome Home!"

When my heart was grieved
>   and my spirit embittered,
I was senseless and ignorant;
>   I was a brute beast before you.
Yet I am always with you;
>   you hold me by my right hand.
You guide me with your counsel,
>   and afterward you will take me into glory.
Whom have I in heaven but you?
>   And earth has nothing I desire besides you.
My flesh and my heart may fail,
>   but God is the strength of my heart
>   and my portion forever.
Those who are far from you will perish;
>   you destroy all who are unfaithful to you.
But as for me, it is good to be near God.
>   I have made the Sovereign LORD my refuge;
>   I will tell of all your deeds.

> —PSALM 73:21–28

The psalmist Asaph affirmed God's presence, that his Father held him and guided him. Asaph realized that everything on Earth that was good came from the hand of the One he desired and who awaited him in Heaven. He affirmed it was good for him to be near God. He made his refuge the Sovereign LORD. What would come at the end of his life? "Afterward you will take me into glory."

My friend Steve Saint told me about the day he and his wife, Ginny, eagerly awaited the arrival of their daughter, twenty-year-old Stephenie, at the Orlando airport after her return from a long trip. With the Saints stood Mincaye, one of the tribal warriors who, in 1956, murdered five missionaries in Ecuador, including Steve's father, Nate. Eventually the gospel that his victims brought to his tribe transformed him. Mincaye became part of the Saint family, with the children calling him Grandfather. At the airport, Grandfather Mincaye waved a sign (upside down) reading Welcome Home, Stephenie.

That night, in the midst of their celebration, Stephenie developed a headache and asked Steve to pray for her. Ginny sat on the bed and held Stephenie, while Steve put his arms around both of them and started praying. While he prayed, Stephenie suffered a massive cerebral hemorrhage. They rushed her to the hospital, where Mincaye saw his beloved Stephenie, whom he called Star, lying on a gurney with a tube down her throat and needles in her arm. He grabbed Steve and said, "Who did this to her?"

"I don't know, Mincaye. Nobody is doing this."

Mincaye grabbed Steve again and said, "Babae, don't you see? God himself is doing this."

Excitedly, Mincaye addressed all the people in the emergency room: "Don't you see? God loving Star, he's taking her to live with him."

Then he told them, "Look at me, I'm an old man; pretty soon I'm going to die too, and I'm going there."

Finally, with a pleading look on his face, Mincaye exhorted these bystanders, "Please, please, won't you follow God's trail too? Coming to God's place, Star and I will be waiting there to welcome you."

Within a few hours, Stephenie died and entered the presence of the Sovereign Lord, whose hand Mincaye recognized in this. I'm confident that when she left this world, a celebration erupted in another world where others, including her Lord and her grandfather Nate Saint, whom she'd never met until then, stretched out their arms and said, "Welcome home, Stephenie."

Father, I don't pretend I wouldn't be distraught at the death of one of my daughters. Surely I would, for I love them so much. But thank you for being sovereign not only when good things happen to us but at all times—good and bad. Thank you for bringing Stephenie safely home and for making it possible for Steve and Ginny, when they die, to see you and her and the great company of your family in a world where we will ever praise you for your goodness and your sovereign grace.

89

Grief Turned to Joy

[Jesus said,] "I tell you the truth, you will weep and mourn
while the world rejoices. You will grieve, but your grief will
turn to joy. A woman giving birth to a child has pain because
her time has come; but when her baby is born she forgets the
anguish because of her joy that a child is born into the world.
So with you: Now is your time of grief, but I will see you again
and you will rejoice, and no one will take away your joy."

—JOHN 16:20–22

A woman giving birth suffers in a way directly connected to
her impending joy. The child comes through suffering, and
therefore the joy of having the child flows out of suffering. Likewise,
God doesn't promise only to *replace our grief with* joy but to *turn it
into* joy.

There's a radical difference between death pangs, which anticipate an ending and look backward, and birth pangs, which anticipate
a beginning and look forward. The old, fallen, cursed Earth, convuls-
ing and groaning in the final pains of childbearing, will birth a

New Earth. Earth will not merely survive; it will live forever, in ever-increasing wonder and glory—as will we, its caretakers, redeemed and birthed through the pains of this present time.

To put your sufferings in perspective, read the biographies of missionaries and reformers such as Martin Luther, John Calvin, William Carey, John Wesley, Charles Spurgeon, Harriet Tubman, William Wilberforce, Hudson Taylor, and numerous others. You'll find their lives riddled with suffering, all of which God used to build their characters and expand their ministries. Rather than depressing us, these stories inspire and challenge us to say no to time-wasting trivia, to seize the day and invest it in what matters. As Robert Moffat said, "We have all eternity to celebrate our victories, but only one short hour before sunset in which to win them."[73]

Jesus said, "I tell you the truth, unless a kernel of wheat falls to the ground and dies, it remains only a single seed. But if it dies, it produces many seeds" (John 12:24). John Piper writes, "A Christian, no matter how dark the season of sadness, never is completely without joy in God. I mean that there remains in his heart the seed of joy in the form, perhaps of only a remembered taste of goodness and an unwillingness to let the goodness go."[74]

God transforms the seeds of suffering into joy. Joy both eclipses and redeems our suffering. And Jesus promises it is a joy that no one can ever take from us.

Lord, remind us that the pains and sorrows of this life are not pains of dying but of childbirth. Something greater and

full of life will not merely replace them but will actually emerge out of them. This means they are purposeful, even when they seem pointless. Just as women, years later, tell stories of childbirth, help us to anticipate living in another world and looking back at this one, then telling our stories of the pains that brought about life. Give us joy now in anticipating Joy, pleasure now in looking forward to Pleasure, peace now in clinging to the eternal Peace purchased with divine blood.

90

Clinging to Christ

The LORD is my light and my salvation—
    whom shall I fear?
The LORD is the stronghold of my life—
    of whom shall I be afraid?
When evil men advance against me
    to devour my flesh,
when my enemies and my foes attack me,
    they will stumble and fall.
Though an army besiege me,
    my heart will not fear;
though war break out against me,
    even then will I be confident.
One thing I ask of the LORD,
    this is what I seek:
that I may dwell in the house of the LORD
    all the days of my life,
to gaze upon the beauty of the LORD
    and to seek him in his temple.
For in the day of trouble
    he will keep me safe in his dwelling;

he will hide me in the shelter of his tabernacle
 and set me high upon a rock.
Then my head will be exalted
 above the enemies who surround me;
at his tabernacle will I sacrifice with shouts of joy;
 I will sing and make music to the LORD.
Hear my voice when I call, O LORD;
 be merciful to me and answer me.
My heart says of you, "Seek his face!"
 Your face, LORD, I will seek.
Do not hide your face from me,
 do not turn your servant away in anger;
 you have been my helper.
Do not reject me or forsake me,
 O God my Savior.
Though my father and mother forsake me,
 the LORD will receive me....
I am still confident of this:
 I will see the goodness of the LORD
 in the land of the living.
Wait for the LORD;
 be strong and take heart
 and wait for the LORD.

—PSALM 27:1–10, 13–14

I n his time of dark suffering, David talks to himself about God's faithfulness and goodness. He encourages himself to trust God and to wait on him. Some self-talk is birthed from the old nature, which speaks contrary to our new nature in Christ. It is like devil-talk, worthy of adamant rejection. But it's always good to listen to self-talk when we speak to ourselves the words of God. This is a habit God's people should cultivate.

Years ago I stopped listening to talk radio. I listen to the Bible instead. Scripture and Bible-based audio books and teaching accompany me as I travel. I never regret investing my time this way—why listen to mere human opinions when you can listen to God? "Man does not live on bread alone but on every word that comes from the mouth of the LORD" (Deuteronomy 8:3).

A woman self-consciously told one of our pastors that before going to sleep each night she reads her Bible, and then she hugs it as she falls asleep. "Is that weird?" she asked. While it may be unusual, it's not weird. This woman has known suffering, and as she clings to his promises, she clings to God. Any father would be moved to hear that his daughter falls asleep with his written words held close to her. Surely God treasures such an act of childlike love.

J. C. Ryle wrote:

There is nothing which shows our ignorance so much as our impatience under trouble. We forget that every cross is a message from God, and intended to do us good in the end. Trials are intended to make us think—to wean us from the world—to send us to the Bible—to drive us to our knees. Health is a good thing but sickness is far better if it leads us to

God. Prosperity is a great mercy; but adversity is a greater one if it brings us to Christ. Anything, anything is better than living in carelessness and dying in sin.[75]

Jesus' tears in the presence of grieving Mary and Martha and his anguish in Gethsemane give us permission and encouragement to cry out to God for deliverance. Jesus didn't want to suffer on the cross, but he said, "Father, if you are willing, take this cup from me; yet not my will, but yours be done" (Luke 22:42).

One day, evil will end. Forever. Suffering and weeping are real and profound, but for God's children, they are temporary. Eternal joy is on its way. God has told us this, and it is a message of great hope and comfort that we should repeat to ourselves every day.

Father, you are there and you are not silent. You have spoken to us. Help us turn off the world's incessant voices so that we may hear you. Help us not only to let you speak to us but to follow David's example in speaking your words to ourselves. We need sanctified self-talk, words of insight and instruction and correction. Help us to seek these in your Word and in what we listen to, read, and watch. With all the voices that cry out for our attention, Lord, help us to turn off and turn away from others' and listen to yours. Then remind us to respeak your words to you, to ourselves, to others, and to the devil whenever he tempts us.

Afterword

The First and Final Word: Jesus

I turned around to see the voice that was speaking to me. And when I turned I saw seven golden lampstands, and among the lampstands was someone "like a son of man," dressed in a robe reaching down to his feet and with a golden sash around his chest. His head and hair were white like wool, as white as snow, and his eyes were like blazing fire. His feet were like bronze glowing in a furnace, and his voice was like the sound of rushing waters. In his right hand he held seven stars, and out of his mouth came a sharp double-edged sword. His face was like the sun shining in all its brilliance.

When I saw him, I fell at his feet as though dead. Then he placed his right hand on me and said: "Do not be afraid. I am the First and the Last. I am the Living One; I was dead, and behold I am alive for ever and ever! And I hold the keys of death and Hades."

—Revelation 1:12–18

When he was taken into Heaven and the apostle John saw Jesus there, he fell on his face like a dead man. He saw the divine glory of the God-man he had walked with upon Earth. Coming from a world of sin, as John did, his entrance into Heaven and the sight of his risen Savior overwhelmed him. The Carpenter from Nazareth was, and will ever be, the King of kings.

About this I am certain: the best answer to the problem of evil and suffering is a person—Jesus Christ. In fact, I'm convinced he is the *only* answer.

In this world that is so torn and shattered, yet still offers remnants and glimpses of beauty and greatness, I have a profound and abiding hope and faith for the future. Not because I follow a set of religious rules to make me better, but because for forty years I've known a real person, and today I know him better than ever. Through inconceivable self-sacrifice, he has touched me deeply, given me a new heart, and utterly transformed my life.

Because he willingly entered this world of evil and suffering and didn't spare himself, but took on the worst of it for my sake and yours, he has earned my trust even for what I can't understand. I and countless others, many of whom have suffered profoundly, have found him to be trustworthy.

He is "the Alpha and the Omega,…the Beginning and the End" (Revelation 22:13).

Scripture gives us many invitations to come to God and personally experience him. The best way to do this is to open the Bible and learn about Jesus. Ask yourself who he is and whether you could believe in him.

Set aside all other arguments and study the person of Christ.

Read of his life in the Gospels, the books of Matthew, Mark, Luke, and John. Listen to his words. Can you look at Jesus and not be broken? Can you gaze on the crucified Christ and still resent God for not doing enough to show his love?

Once you see Jesus as he really is, your worldview, your goals, your affections, *everything*—including your view of evil and suffering—will change.

Jesus asked his disciples the most important question: *"Who do you say I am?"* (Matthew 16:15). If we get it right about Jesus, we can afford to get some minor things wrong. But if we get it wrong about Jesus, it won't matter in the end what else we get right.

When it comes to goodness and evil, present suffering and eternal joy, the first Word and the last is Jesus.

Notes

1. Sinclair B. Ferguson, *Deserted by God?* (Grand Rapids, MI: Baker Books, 1993), 51.

2. C. S. Lewis, *A Grief Observed* (Whitstable, Kent, UK: Whitstable Litho, 1966), 31.

3. James Boice, sermon, Tenth Presbyterian Church, Philadelphia, PA, May 7, 2000, SingleVision Ministries, www.seegod.org/boice_example.htm (accessed May 2, 2009).

4. Charles Haddon Spurgeon, *Christian History* 10, no. 1 (1991): 29.

5. Jonathan Aitken, *John Newton: From Disgrace to Amazing Grace* (Wheaton, IL: Crossway Books, 2007), 347.

6. Charles Haddon Spurgeon, *The Autobiography of Charles H. Spurgeon* (Grand Rapids, MI: Revell, 1899), 76.

7. Scott Hahn, *A Father Who Keeps His Promises* (Cincinnati: St. Anthony Messenger Press, 1998), 13–14.

8. ABC7, WLS-TV, Chicago, April 7, 1998, news report; *Through the Flames* book description, www.crossway.org/product/663575724360.

9. Thomas E. Schmidt, *Trying to Be Good* (Grand Rapids, MI: Zondervan, 1990), 180–83, quoted in William Lane Craig, *Hard Questions, Real Answers* (Wheaton, IL: Crossway Books, 2003), 109–10.

10. Harold S. Kushner, *When Bad Things Happen to Good People* (New York: Schocken Books, 1981), 134.

11. Corrie ten Boom, interview with Pat Robertson on *The 700 Club*, 1974, YouTube, www.youtube.com/watch?v=6VZYFDCS3G w&NR=1 (accessed July 24, 2010).

12. C. S. Lewis, *The Lion, the Witch and the Wardrobe* (New York: HarperCollins, 1978), 80.

13. C. S. Lewis, *The Problem of Pain* (New York: Macmillan, 1962), 40–41.

14. Lewis, *The Problem of Pain*, 40.

15. John Donne, *Sermons,* 3:751, quoted in Randy Alcorn, *Heaven* (Carol Stream, IL: Tyndale, 2004), 165.

16. Ann Stump, video, November 22, 1997, Eternal Perspective Ministries, www.epm.org/resources/2010/Feb/8/ann-stumps-testimony/ (accessed July 24, 2010).

17. Lewis, *The Lion, the Witch and the Wardrobe,* 151–55.

18. Dorothy L. Sayers, "The Greatest Drama Ever Staged," in *The Whimsical Christian* (New York: Collier Macmillan, 1987), 12.

19. John R. W. Stott, *The Cross of Christ* (Downers Grove, IL: InterVarsity, 1986), 327.

20. Timothy Keller, *The Reason for God* (New York: Dutton, 2008), 30.

21. Keller, *The Reason for God,* 31.

22. Vicki Anderson, "Hypertelorism," About Face Blog, http://aboutfacenow.blogspot.com/2005/01/hypertelorism_23.html; and "Deformed Face Myths," About Face Blog, http://aboutfacenow.blogspot.com/2006/09/deformed-face-myths.html (accessed July 24, 2010).

23. John D. Woodbridge, *Great Leaders of the Christian Church* (Chicago: Moody, 1989), 344.

24. Benjamin Breckinridge Warfield, *Faith and Life* (Edinburgh, Scotland: Banner of Truth, 1991), 20.

25. Malcolm Muggeridge, *A Twentieth Century Testimony* (Nashville: Thomas Nelson, 1978).

26. Lewis, *The Problem of Pain*, 33–34.

27. Joni Eareckson Tada and Steven Estes, *When God Weeps* (Grand Rapids, MI: Zondervan, 1997), 83.

28. C. S. Lewis, *Letters of C. S. Lewis* (Orlando: Harcourt Books, 1966), 477.

29. Dinesh D'Souza, *What's So Great About Christianity?* (Washington, D.C.: Regnery, 2007), 291.

30. F. F. Bruce, *The Epistle of Paul to the Romans* (Downers Grove, IL: InterVarsity, 1985), 168.

31. J. R. R. Tolkien, *The Return of the King* (New York: Random House, 1973), 247.

32. Tada and Estes, *When God Weeps*, 216.

33. Lewis, *The Problem of Pain*, 128.

34. Michael Wilson, "Flight 1549 Pilot Tells of Terror and Intense Focus," *New York Times*, February 9, 2009.

35. Barbara Brown Taylor, "On Not Being God," *Review and Expositor* 99, no. 4 (Fall 2002): 611.

36. Charles Haddon Spurgeon, "A Heavenly Pattern for Our Earthly Life," Sermon 1778, April 30, 1884, The Spurgeon Archive, www.spurgeon.org/sermons/1778.htm (accessed July 24, 2010).

37. See Philip Yancey and Paul Brand, *Fearfully and Wonderfully Made* (Grand Rapids, MI: Zondervan, 1997).

38. Lewis, *The Problem of Pain*, 116.

39. Nancy Guthrie, *Holding On to Hope* (Carol Stream, IL: Tyndale, 2002), 9.

40. Guthrie, *Holding On to Hope,* 10.

41. Aggie Hurst, "A Story of Eternal Perspective," Eternal Perspective Ministries, www.epm.org/resources/2010/Feb/18/story-eternal-perspective/ (accessed July 24, 2010).

42. Alice Gray, *Treasures for Women Who Hope* (Nashville: Thomas Nelson, 2005), 71–72.

43. Adapted from Gray, *Treasures for Women Who Hope,* 51–52.

44. Nick Vujicic, "A Remarkable Story of God's Grace," Life Without Limbs, www.lifewithoutlimbs.org/about-nick-vujicic.php%20 (accessed July 24, 2010).

45. Tada and Estes, *When God Weeps,* 117.

46. Personal letter from Ethel Herr. Used by permission.

47. Fanny Crosby, *Fanny Crosby's Life-Story* (New York: Every Where, 1903), 13–14.

48. Josef Ton (also Tson), *Suffering, Martyrdom, and Rewards in Heaven* (Lanham, MD: University Press of America, 1997), 429.

49. Ajith Fernando, *A Call to Joy and Pain* (Wheaton, IL: Crossway Books, 2007), 77–78.

50. Elisabeth Elliot, *A Path Through Suffering* (Ann Arbor, MI: Servant Publications, 1990), 154–55.

51. Richard Baxter, "The Cure of Melancholy and Overmuch Sorrow, by Faith," Puritan Sermons, www.puritansermons.com/baxter/baxter25.htm (accessed July 24, 2010).

52. Corrie ten Boom, *The Hiding Place* (Grand Rapids, MI: Chosen Books, 2006), 210, 220.

53. Charles Spurgeon, *An All-Round Ministry* (Edinburgh: The

Banner of Truth Trust, 1960), 384; as cited by John Piper in his sermon "Charles Spurgeon: Preaching Through Adversity," 1995 Bethlehem Conference for Pastors, http://desiringgod.org/ResourceLibrary/Biographies/1469_Charles_Spurgeon_Preaching_Through_Adversity/.

54. Charles Spurgeon, quoted in Darrel W. Amundsen, "The Anguish and Agonies of Charles Spurgeon," in *Christian History* 10, no. 1:25; as cited by John Piper in his sermon "Charles Spurgeon: Preaching Through Adversity," 1995 Bethlehem Conference for Pastors, http://desiringgod.org/ResourceLibrary/Biographies/1469_ Charles_Spurgeon_Preaching_Through_Adversity/.

55. Samuel Rutherford, *Letters of Samuel Rutherford,* quoted in Joni Eareckson Tada and Steven Estes, *A Step Further* (Grand Rapids, MI: Zondervan, 1990), 179.

56. Richard Baxter, *The Saints' Everlasting Rest,* ed. John Thomas Wilkinson (Grand Rapids, MI: Baker Book House, 1978), 246.

57. Lewis, *The Problem of Pain,* 93.

58. Thornton Wilder, *The Collected Short Plays of Thornton Wilder, Vol. II,* (New York: Theatre Communications Group, 1998).

59. Jon Tal Murphee, *A Loving God and a Suffering World* (Downers Grove, IL: InterVarsity Press, 1981), 115.

60. Doug Wolter, "Justin, Dustin, and God's Lessons on Suffering," September 21, 2007, Life Together Blog, http://life2getherblog.com/2007/09/25/justin-dustin-and-gods-lessons-in-suffering/ (accessed July 24, 2010).

61. Joni Eareckson Tada, True Women Conference, October 10, 2008.

62. E. Stanley Jones, *A Song of Ascents* (Nashville: Abingdon, 1968), 180.

63. Richard Wurmbrand, *Tortured for Christ* (Bartlesville, OK: Living Sacrifice Book Co., 1990), 57.

64. Michael Card, "Wounded in the House of Friends," *Virtue,* March–April 1991, 28–29, 69.

65. Elisabeth Elliot, *A Path Through Suffering,* 151–52.

66. I devote a chapter to my friendship with Jerry in my book *In Light of Eternity: Perspectives on Heaven* (Colorado Springs: Water-Brook, 1999), 66–72.

67. Patti Franklin, "Ordinary People in Extraordinary Times," Eternal Perspective Ministries, www.epm.org/resources/2010/Apr/15/ordinary-people-extraordinary-times/ (accessed July 24, 2010).

68. Kenneth Samuel Wuest, *Word Studies in the Greek New Testament* (Grand Rapids, MI: Eerdmans, 1980), 235.

69. Joseph Bayly, *Psalms of My Life* (Colorado Springs: David C. Cook, 2002). Used with permission of the Bayly family.

70. First part of quote from Helen Keller, *The World I Live In* (New York: New York Review of Books, 2004), 130; second part, "Believe…" from Helen Keller, *We Bereaved* (New York: L. Fulenwider, 1929).

71. Joni Eareckson Tada, "Hope…the Best of Things," in John Piper and Justin Taylor, *Suffering and the Sovereignty of God* (Wheaton, IL: Crossway Books, 2006), 195.

72. Tada and Estes, *When God Weeps,* 196–97.

73. Robert Moffat, quoted in *Eternities: Webster's Quotations, Facts and Phrases* (San Diego: ICON Group, 2008), 3.

74. John Piper, *When I Don't Desire God* (Wheaton, IL: Crossway Books, 2004), 220.

75. J. C. Ryle, *Ryle's Expository Thoughts on the Gospels* (New York: R. Carter & Brothers, 1879), 180.

About the Author

R ANDY ALCORN is the founder and director of Eternal Perspective Ministries (EPM). Prior to 1990, when he started EPM, he served as a pastor for fourteen years. He has spoken around the world and has taught on the adjunct faculties of Multnomah University and Western Seminary in Portland, Oregon.

Randy is the best-selling author of thirty-some books with five million in print in twenty-eight languages. Randy has written for many magazines and produces the popular periodical *Eternal Perspectives*. He's been a guest on over seven hundred radio and television programs including *Focus on the Family, The Bible Answer Man, Family Life Today, Revive Our Hearts,* and *Truths That Transform.*

The father of two married daughters, Karina and Angela, Randy lives in Gresham, Oregon, with his wife and best friend, Nanci. They are the proud grandparents of four grandsons: Jake, Matt, Ty, and Jack. Randy enjoys hanging out with his family, biking, tennis, research, and reading.

You may contact Eternal Perspective Ministries by e-mail through its Web site at www.epm.org or at 39085 Pioneer Blvd., Suite 206, Sandy, OR 97055, (503) 668-5200 or toll free 877-376-4567.

Connect with Randy Alcorn for his daily thoughts at
www.facebook.com/randyalcorn
www.twitter.com/randyalcorn

Visit Randy Alcorn's blog at www.epm.org/blog.

Deepen Your Faith in God's Goodness

Randy Alcorn diligently tackles the toughest questions about suffering, evil and the goodness of God to uncover the hopeful truth from the only reliable source—the Bible. Increase your understanding of this complex topic and equip yourself to share your faith more clearly in this world of pain and fear.

Special introductory booklet, available as a 10-pack. Randy Alcorn takes on the key questions we can't escape when we search for God amidst the suffering and evil before us. Ideal for distribution to grief support group members or as a gift for a loved one struggling with loss.

Three study guides in one.
- The four-week study is an overview of the key points of *If God Is Good* and how they reveal a character of God that is loving and comforting in times of trouble.
- The eight-week study is an advanced course that probes the theological arguments in *If God Is Good,* including the sovereignty of God, the problem of evil, and the existence of God.
- The thirteen-week study is structured for use as a church sermon series and Sunday school discussions.
- Includes Leaders' guide.

In this specially condensed adaptation of *If God Is Good,* Alcorn confronts issues that are far from simple and provides answers that are far from easy. He shows how the way of suffering—a path that Jesus himself knew better than anyone else—can ultimately become a journey into wholeness and even logic-defying joy.